Praise for *B*

This book is truly a breakthrough; a hope-filled epistle to the modern church in a rapidly changing world. Rev. Dr. Weaks captures the spirit of courage and resilience necessary to build effective and connected ministry that meets people where they are with the love of Christ. I said "amen" and "hallelujah" aloud a few times while reading this powerful story, and I bet you will, too. —Rev. Erin Wathen, Pastor, Grace Immanuel United Church of Christ and author of *Resist and Persist: Faith and the Fight for Equality*

In a time when many pastors and congregations are struggling, this book is right on time. Dawn Darwin Weaks' book, *Breakthrough*, is an encouraging word that will uplift, inspire, challenge, and surprise you. She shares a down-to-earth story of church growth that honors relationships, trust, risk-taking, loving one another, and loving our neighbors who are most in need. It's a story of good news for the church. —Sarah Griffith Lund, Senior Pastor, First Congregational of Indianapolis, IN, author, and national staff, United Church of Christ

For anyone who's ever felt cynical about church, *Breakthrough* is a breath of fresh air: the real-life story of a congregation who chose not to stay stuck, but to hear the Spirit's whisper, then take a giant leap of faith. By sharing her church's story, Weaks invites us all to dream about what bold faithfulness might look like in our own contexts, but more than that, she inspires us to believe those dreams might be possible. —Rev. Kyndall Rae Rothaus, author of *Thy Queendom Come: Breaking Free from the Patriarchy to Save Your Soul*

Weaks has poignantly captured how to do change well. Readers will be captivated by the story, but take away lessons for engaging change in their own context. For any congregation going through a challenging time, this is the book for you. —F. Douglas Powe, Jr., Director, Lewis Center at Wesley Theological Seminary and James C. Logan Professor of Evangelism

For years, churches have abided by the real estate adage, "location, location, location." In telling the story of a dying downtown congregation that relocated, pastors Dawn and Joe Weaks tell how it's not just where a church can be found, but what it means to *be* church that really matters. Theirs now meets at "the intersection of Inclusive and Purposeful." This book is full of practical *and* theological wisdom. A must-read for every dying church looking to be resurrected! —Mike Graves, Wm. K. McElvaney Professor of Preaching and Worship emeritus, Saint Paul School of Theology and Scholar in Residence, Country Club Christian Church

Dawn's book is no pollyannaish "this will be the answer for every congregation." Rather it's the story of the callings perceived and acted upon in one congregation. Here is applied ecclesiology - recognizing when a congregation needs to relocate, remodel, re-engage one's community. Her style visualizes the process. The story can be rejuvenating! —Bill Tillman, Coordinator of the Center for Congregational Ethics

No matter where your church is in its life cycle, change is both chilling and thrilling. With *Breakthrough*, Pastor Dawn Darwin Weaks leads us through the story of one church's journey that is less a blueprint to follow than a spirit to be caught. Dawn, her co-pastor and husband Joe Weaks, and many congregational voices speak hope to us through these pages. Their creative and purposeful work is a balm and a blessing. —Rev. Dr. George A. Mason, Senior Pastor, Wilshire Baptist Church, Dallas, Texas

This book is a blessing. "Be of good courage and be encouraged" I hear Jesus say through the different voices in this book. With Rev. Dawn Weaks serving as the main narrator, joined by the first-person stories and insights of others in the church, we get to hear the multi-faceted story of one church's adventure in following the call to serve Jesus. This church bravely took stock of where they were, where the Holy Spirit was calling them to be, and how they might get from the first place to the second. With humility, honesty, and humor we follow them from their old historic downtown building, to a wine bar, to a restaurant, to an elementary school. In true Exodus-style, these nomads in the wilderness learned that God still tabernacles, sets up shop for a time here and a time there, revealing Godself in myriad ways and blessing people in the most holy, if unlikely ways along the Way. This is a church that prays, studies Scripture, and, therefore, stays connected to the love of God concretely and palpably. We see their hopes, their fears, their disagreements, and their grief at what had to be laid to rest in order for resurrection to break forth. They now inhabit a "permanent" space (as if any church location were truly permanent) in which they partner with other nonprofits to greater effect for their community. They have mastered "doing church in weird places." There is no doubt the reader will get genuinely excited to consider what might be possible for their *own* church community if "Fearless" became the theme for a year. We, too, might break new ground, holy ground, where we connect in life-giving ways. As Rev. Weaks declares and her church models richly for us: "God's blessings must come not only *to* you, but *through* you to truly be divine blessing." Amen. —Rev. Dr. Jaime Clark-Soles, Perkins School of Theology, Southern Methodist University

Breakthrough

TRUSTING GOD FOR BIG CHANGE IN YOUR CHURCH

Dawn Darwin Weaks

**chalice
press**

Saint Louis, Missouri

An imprint of Christian Board of Publication

Scripture quotations are translated by Joe Weaks, Ph.D.

Print ISBN 9780827203280
EPUB 9780827203297
EPDF 9780827203303

ChalicePress.com

Printed in Canada

Foreword

Every few weeks or so, we get another phone call or email. "We heard you made big changes at your church and it's working out well," they say. "Would you tell us about it?" At first, I jotted some of our church's story down just to have an in-house history of God's crazy-good faithfulness. But the more people asked for our story, the more I wanted to have something to give them so I could say, "Read this and then we'll talk." That's how this little book came to be. Because if our church's story can help other churches thrive, I'm all in. I still believe that the best way to share the gospel of Jesus Christ that gives hope to our world is through a community committed to following him. That's right, the church.

I asked our church's leaders how they felt about sharing our story more broadly. They enthusiastically endorsed the idea. However, some were a little surprised when I asked them to add their voices to the book! But when I explained that God moved through all of us working together, especially them, and most definitely not just me, they reluctantly agreed. They are some of the best Christian people ever. I think you'll see why I think so. Also, my husband and co-pastor Joe's voice had to show up occasionally in my telling of the story, just like it would if we were sitting around your dining room table. He's half the pastoral team that led this transformation and a whole lot of my heart.

But the voice I really want you to hear in this story is God's own voice, coming to you. That's why there are questions to ponder and scripture to read from Luke's gospel at the end of this book. Ideally, you and some church friends will lay our story beside yours, add the biblical stories too, then, look at it until you see something new. You very likely will. That's how creative and dependable the Holy Spirit is. May you be ready to move when you get that holy nudge. Here's what happened when we did.

*for Arwen Ruth and Sam Allen, best double preachers' kids ever,
who turned out more than okay*

Contents

Acknowledgments   viii

Chapter 1: Before   1

Chapter 2: Too Late?   7

Chapter 3: Church in Weird Places   15

Chapter 4 : Fearless   23

Chapter 5: The Requirement for Resurrection   29

Chapter 6: A Blast from the Past   39

Chapter 7: Clink, Clink, Clink   45

Chapter 8 : The Cafetorium Wilderness   51

Chapter 9: The Key Ingredient   59

Chapter 10: Y'all Means All   65

Chapter 11: Where Does It Hurt?   73

Chapter 12: Drive-In Church   81

Chapter 13: Surprised to Thrive   89

Chapter 14: After   95

Small Group Guide   99

Acknowledgements

I don't know how to thank a whole congregation of amazing people for being fearless and faithful. I am so grateful to be one of the pastors of Connection Christian Church in Odessa, Texas! Also, I am not sure if I am just foolish to tell their story while I am still employed as their pastor, or maybe if I am just super trusting, but here goes. It's simply too good to keep. Thank you especially to the church members who wrote their testimonies for this book; you said it better than I ever could. Thank you too, to all of those church members whose names aren't mentioned here in print but whose behind-the-scenes faithfulness propelled, and still propels, our church forward. I'm also grateful to the folks at Chalice Press, to Indu Guzman, Rebecca Bowman Woods, Kevin Neece, and especially Brad Lyons, for believing in the Church and the power of our congregation to encourage other congregations with God's help. I'm grateful for dear colleagues who read the manuscript and offered their invaluable feedback. And I have a debt I'll never be able to repay to the ministers who pastored this congregation before me. We reap the fruit of the seeds others sowed. Especially big thanks go to our grown kids who went on this whole adventure with us, adding so much of their own love and energy. And most of all, thank you to Joe Weaks, my partner and colleague, who always gives me the senior minister's office and is my 24/7 helpline— and not just as technical support. But that too.

Hasn't God been good?

CHAPTER 1

Before

God is all about the too old, the too late, and the too dead. From the birth of Isaac to elderly Sarah and Abraham in Genesis to the resurrection of Jesus in the gospels, it's when things look bleak that God's powerful love is easiest to see at work. That's why our congregation dared to place our 110-year-old, slowly dying church into the hands of God, whose other name is "Surprise!"[1] This book tells you what happened when we did. Our story is for those who feel the air getting stale in their churches and hope for something more. It's for those who wonder if it's time to close the doors on God's work through their church. And most of all, this book is for those who dare to imagine where a new window might open if that door were to close.

I'm not telling you our church's story and introducing you to our congregational leaders so that your church can do exactly what we did. It doesn't work that way! Your situation is unique and different from ours. Therefore, in these pages, you will not find a snazzy program to follow. You most certainly will not find heroic pastors to emulate! You will also not find a special, secret, theological sauce that makes the magic happen. Instead, you *will* find gritty, well-grounded hope. Because while our churches may be different, our God is the same. So, you can have hope! Hope that our God still moves through the church. Hope that from the historical foundations of our congregations, the Holy Spirit can fashion a new future. Hope that God's plan for sharing the gospel of Jesus Christ still happens through the people in the pews—or the people in the chairs. Let's start there.

---

[1] John Claypool, "God's Other Name is Surprise," lecture at the Whitworth Institute of Ministry, Whitworth, WA, courtesy of the Northwest Digital Archives, August 23, 1985.

The summer I was fourteen years old, I was sitting outside on a metal folding chair during a church camp worship service. I remember the chair because it was the only thing cool on that hot July night. The preacher, who seemed old and gray to me at the time but probably was my age now, preached about God's blessings. I still remember one of the sermon's lines, "A blessing from God needs to pass *through* you, not just *to* you, if it's going to remain a blessing from God." As the preacher talked, suddenly, I felt like God was singling me out. It seemed like God wanted me to do something. It was not a voice, not an audible one at least. It was like the Holy Spirit just touched my shoulder somehow. Before I knew it, I was walking to the front of the worship service. I passed dozens of kids still seated in their cool metal folding chairs as I leapt into the heat of the unknown. I couldn't say why I was moving up front exactly. I only knew I had to say "Yes."

It had not, up to that point, occurred to me to be a minister. My dad was one. My mom had gone to seminary for a bit. I'd known women who were children's ministers and chaplains. The Baptist church I grew up in had women deacons, a rare thing. Back then, none of that ministry stuff had crossed my mind as something for me. Yet that night, I experienced the most urgent impression that God was calling me. To what, I did not know.

I'd been baptized when I was six years old, and had thought of myself as a Christian since then, so this wasn't about a confession of faith. When I made it up front to the preacher, I didn't know what to say, so I just said to him, "I think God is telling me to do something." He smiled, patted my back, and gestured for me to sit down on the front row of chairs. I did. The service ended, and that was it.

That moment may have faded into the background with all my other camp memories, if it weren't for Patty. I was a little befuddled about what to do, even where to go, after this seemingly holy nudge. People started packing up the folding chairs and shuffling off to the nightly camp games. But Patty, a 20-something seminary student, came over and sat beside me there on the front row. She said to me, "I saw what happened to you tonight. Did God speak to you?" I tentatively nodded yes. It felt very strange to claim such a thing had happened to me. Once Patty acknowledged my experience, I was comforted, but still frightened. Patty said, "I want you to write today's date down in your Bible and put what you felt and heard. That way you will never doubt that this actually happened to you. You will always know that God called you." So that night back in the dorms I crawled up on my top bunk. After the counselor hollered for lights out, I grabbed my flashlight. I fished my Bible and pen out from under my pillow and dove in. "June 26, 1986. God called me and I said Yes," I wrote, and then tucked my confession back under my pillow. That now-tattered Bible with my scribbled Ebenezer has helped me in many an uncertain, despairing moment. It was real. God did call and I did answer. It's right there in ink, thanks to Patty.

It was a really good thing I wrote that down. The opposing winds were pretty brutal. What to me was a life-changing moment was often dismissed. As a female, I did not have the proper anatomical equipment to be taken seriously by very many. Meanwhile, I began the life-long process of weaning away from others' approval. I girded up my loins as I graduated from high school in 1989 and headed to college as a student of "full-time ministry."

About that same time in the oil patch of West Texas, First Christian Church of Odessa held a congregational meeting. The church was deciding if they would call their first woman to be an elder. In the Christian Church (Disciples of Christ) denomination, elders are the primary spiritual leaders of the church. Marita Hendrick, a lovely dark-haired woman always decked out in turquoise and a no-nonsense, can-do attitude, was nominated as the first woman elder in the church's 80-year history. Marita had earned the trust of the congregation over the decades by doing every job available to women at the time. When she agreed to be nominated, a couple of men tried to get her to back down. They told her that women in leadership would ruin the church. According to them, men wouldn't volunteer anymore if they knew women would do it! Marita simply reminded the men that they were her friends and nothing would change that. And, she said, didn't they remember the church had women leaders from the start? She was right. Years ago, the women in the church had rallied to raise funds for the church when all it had was dirt for a floor. Women selling their chickens' eggs and baked goods from their own kitchens were the reason the congregation even had a place to stand! Marita stood her ground and the congregational vote was held. It was decided by an overwhelming but not unanimous vote: First Christian Church in Odessa, Texas would have women elders!

An incident decades earlier had prepared the congregation for making this stride toward the full inclusion of all people. That time, God moved through someone who *wouldn't* get out of his chair! In the 1950s, the Christian Church (Disciples of Christ) began to split between "Independent" Christians and "Brotherhood" Christians. In essence the division was about interpretation of scripture. Independent Christians wanted a narrower range of acceptable interpretation. The Brotherhood wanted to maintain room for the conscience of each person to interpret the Bible as each one felt led. Ironically, the "Brotherhood" became known for advancing women's equality based on scriptures that they interpreted as supportive of women's leadership. Many churches were dealing with this tug of war between understandings of the Bible. First Christian Church of Odessa was one of them.

The pastor at the time insisted upon the church going with the "Independent" branch in that denominational split. He saw the Bible in a more narrowly defined way. The elders disagreed, and prayerful dialogue seemingly failed. At the next elders' meeting, this pastor insisted that the church would join the "Independent" split from the denomination. He would not budge on his convictions, and the elders decided that was enough. They told the pastor that his time with this church was over. They asked him to pack up and depart. But he refused to leave. So, the story goes, two of the burlier elders went over to the pastor's chair, and picked it up. With him in it! A third elder held the door. They then sat the pastor, still in his chair, outside the building, in the alley. And they locked the door behind him! That very night, they changed the locks themselves.

From that moment on, First Christian Church displayed an unshakeable commitment to being a place of freedom of conscience and loyalty to the "Brotherhood" which became the Christian Church (Disciples of Christ) denomination. Those elders, who took their shepherding role as protectors of the sheep very seriously, paved the way for strong congregational leaders, both male and female, to come. They and those who had come before them set the expectation that the pastor would not run the church; rather, a partnership of congregational leaders and pastors was the way the church would move forward. They would not allow the pastor to dictate how the congregation was to understand scripture. Instead, they would make room for each person to grow in their understanding and interpretation as they matured in faith and connected in community. Thanks be to God!

Thirty years after that chair incident, the congregation decided women could be in any leadership role in the church. Marita became an elder, and later, the church confirmed her as the first female board chairperson. Meanwhile, I went from church camp to studying for ministry. I did not yet know that women could even be pastors; I was just trying to stay faithful to the "yes" I gave that propelled me off my folding chair and down the aisle. Marita paved the way for me, though she didn't know it at the time. That's why this book is not about hot shot pastors who followed a fancy program and turned their church around. This book is about courageous, unpaid, nonprofessional, dedicated congregational leaders who turned their church around, and the pastors who received the blessing of witnessing their moxie along the way. I am one of those pastors. So is my husband, Joe.

Another connection was beginning during those blue eyeshadow, big-hair 1980s when the church began to call women to serve in all leadership positions. My now co-pastor and husband Joe was growing up in the Houston area. His dad Rick was working in a steel mill. When Rick got laid off in the steel crash of the early 1980s, he went to work as a mail carrier. And it just so happened that the First Christian Church in Baytown, Texas, had a mighty fine water fountain on his route. When Rick delivered mail there, he would often grab a quick drink of water from their fountain. Rick suggested that the family try out the church with the good water fountain.

Soon after, Joe was baptized in that church. He was fully immersed into church life: choir, youth group, the church softball team, and of course, camps. The mentoring he received at camp made him think about becoming a minister. By the time Joe graduated from high school, he too sensed a call to ministry. He and I hadn't met yet, but our trajectory of connection was beginning.

Have you ever noticed that watching God work often happens best in hindsight? Sometimes we as church leaders are working so hard to get past the past, we may overlook God's powerful graces in it. The Holy Spirit was weaving connections long before we were aware it was happening: connections for Joe and I to meet each other, for us both to be able to serve this historied congregation, and for our community to be reached by the gospel through our church in the twenty-first century. In 2014, Joe and I came to serve First Christian Church in Odessa as its co-pastors. Though we had some steep challenges ahead, we praised the Lord for all of the foundations that others had laid over the years.

And mostly, we prayed we never would have to be carried out in a chair!

In Their Words by Marita Hendrick

It was a time in our church's history, the 1980s, when women were not accepted in leadership positions. I was honored to have been asked to be an elder, the first woman elder. There was a lot of grumbling among the older men and women in our congregation. We even lost some members because they didn't think women should have a place at the communion table or, for that matter, in any leadership role. But the church pressed on, and I was elected.

A couple of years later we progressed even more, and I was asked to be the chairperson of our church board. That was the last thing some of our older gentlemen wanted, and they told me so. I joked around with them during that year, trying to ease their doubts, and before that year was over, they told me that while it had not been what they had expected, I had been a very good board chairman. That was the highest compliment I could have received from them.

I am delighted that things have changed. We have women serving in many areas of our church and have seven very capable women elders serving currently. Our church has gone through many changes in the past few years. I am so proud of our church for being a leader in our community, and probably, in the state of Texas. We look forward to future years knowing that God will show us the way.

CHAPTER 2
Too Late?

In the summer of 2014, Joe and I drove our Honda Civic into the back parking lot of the funeral home in our Kansas City suburb. Thankfully no bereaved families were gathering, so we got a spot in the shade on this sweltering, ain't-no-humid-like-Missouri-humid July evening. He cut the engine and rolled down the windows. We looked each other in the eye and took a deep breath, waiting to see who would speak first. I settled into the sweltering silence and thought, *how did we get here?*

When we were in seminary in Fort Worth, Texas, Joe and I were study buddies and occasional dance partners on group trips to Billy Bob's, a famous honkytonk. We could cut a rug together, Joe with his strong leading and my (only on the dance floor) following. But we swore off ever dating each other. "Who wants to marry another minister?" we said. Too complicated. About two years into our friendship, we started to realize neither of us had been dating anyone else for a while. We began to think this might be something. After we married, each of us pastored our own churches separately for several years. Then, when our babies came along, we considered co-pastoring. One day while on a plane to interview for a co-pastorate opportunity, we used a cocktail napkin to write down all the tasks a pastor does. Then we marked which we thought were our individual strengths. Whatd'ya know? Put together, we nearly made one complete pastor!

Kansas City, Missouri, became our first co-pastorate. The longest I've lived anywhere was in that split-level Midwestern house on a tree-lined street in the neighborhood our kids will always remember as their childhood home. After nine years there, the phone rang in my church office. A persuasive, West Texan, Disciples of Christ elder named Amy Hendrick was on the other end. Her drawl and wit reminded me of my Texas family and friends. She wanted Joe and me to consider a move to co-pastor her 108-year-old congregation in Odessa, Texas. She talked about what it means to be a Disciples of Christ church in a Baptist town. She said the congregation was ready to take risks to be a vibrant blessing to the community. I had rarely heard a congregational leader speak so astutely about the identity of her church and our denomination. I was mildly intrigued, but still reluctant, because we were happy and comfortable right where we were.

Amy didn't give up easily though. A note in the mail here, a phone call from their church's current interim minister there, and eventually, this determined search committee's enthusiasm convinced us to make a visit. Now, Odessa is a flat, nearly treeless, oil-field town. Like the song from the hit Broadway musical *Dear Evan Hansen*, "all we see is sky for forever."[2] Well, sky and pumpjacks, the most visible part of an oil well. The joke is that if you want someone to take a job in Odessa, you've got to fly them in at night. That way they can get a first impression before realizing what the landscape looks like. But they brought us to visit in broad daylight. I remember seeing the fields of cacti on the road out of the airport and thinking, *Toto, we are not in Kansas (City) anymore!* Once we arrived at the hotel, a huge gift basket with local treats like "Texas trash" candy awaited us in our top-floor room. Nice touch, I thought. Together, Joe and I looked out our hotel window over the city. I said to him, "It's not as bad as I thought it would be!?"

Over the next two days, we visited church members' homes and ate at some great restaurants. We talked with local city and school leaders as part of our introduction to the area. We were visiting during an oil boom when everything seemed possible. The energy, the traffic, and the price of oil were very high. The housing market was such that if a house was listed on a Tuesday, it would have nine offers on it by Wednesday, at far above the appraisal value. Everyone seemed to sense both the potential and problems that come with overcrowding. We caught the intoxicating spirit.

The people on the search committee couldn't be beat. They were kind, funny, smart, and genuine Jesus-lovers. Maybe best of all was Jackie

---

[2] Benj Pasek and Justin Paul, "For Forever," *Dear Evan Hansen*, Theatre Communications Group, 2017.

Sue Barnes, who was the Ector County clerk for many years, and had been a member of this church for her entire life. Her family roots were a part of the history of the area. Jackie Sue was teeny-tiny in stature and huge in personality. Now in her 80s, her emphysema made it hard for her to get her breath now and then, but that did not stop her. She regaled us with tales of Odessa and the church's history, her blue eyes twinkling with mischief and kindness. As she prayed the blessing over our mid-afternoon margaritas on a restaurant patio, I thought to myself, "I'd like to be in a church that grows people like Jackie Sue."

We enjoyed these folks, and we could see ourselves in Odessa, more so than we would've guessed. It was a pleasant surprise. But the real test was to come. On one of the last stops on our tour, the search committee took us to the church's two buildings. In broad daylight. And our hearts sank.

The frog in the kettle adage never seemed truer. This congregation was trying to be the church on a dusty corner one block off success. In fact, the story goes that a beloved pastor during the 1950s once regretted that a lightning bolt struck the Methodist church nearby, causing a fire. "If only it had struck us," legend recalls him lamenting, "We so badly need a new location." Sixty years later, downtown Odessa still was not a happening place. But it was especially not happening in this off-the-beaten-path spot. Maybe they had already waited too long to make radical changes to save this church's ministry. The deferred maintenance on these beloved old buildings was daunting.

Especially damning to the health of the church was the alley that ran between the two buildings. Since the construction of the "new" sanctuary building during the church's heyday in the 1960s, parents had been expected to carry their babies across the alley to the nursery in the 1940s-era building. Then they would return to worship in the 1960s era building, leaving their children two decades behind across the alley. Very few families with children were active in the church anymore. Most worrisome of all, the church was living off its endowment fund, drawing it down more each year, and still not able to maintain the buildings. The writing was on the wall.

The congregational leadership knew something needed to change. They had watched the church's attendance, giving, and community impact decline for over a decade. Proactively, they were trying some new things. They had started a new contemporary service with their previous pastor, but the attendance was poor. They also had strongly considered merging with the sister church they had started sixty years ago. The two churches had even combined youth ministries for a couple of years. In the end, however, the other church did not want to merge.

Another option they explored was combining forces with two other declining mainline churches in town. Leaders from the three churches held on-and-off-again, informal conversations about merging their congregations and starting something completely new. That was an exciting prospect. But thinking about what to do with three churches' assets, not to mention personalities, in order to combine them was too overwhelming to fathom. Sadly, each congregation concluded they would keep giving it another old college try on their own. But First Christian knew that something more would be needed, somehow, someway. They were looking to a new pastor for direction.

Joe and I were not going to mince words. Many downtown churches with old buildings are worth remodeling and relaunching right there in that spot. Perhaps there is a vibrant community living nearby to reach, if only the church wants to position itself for growth. This was not that. Some work was being done on downtown revitalization, some distant talk of lofts or apartments being built, but that was at least a decade away from fruition. This church might not make it that long. It might already be too late as it was. So, for our last conversation with the search committee, Joe and I gave the tough news.

"We think this church needs to move to a new location," we said. "Our hunch is that the buildings are not worth remodeling where you are."

They all looked at each other and swallowed hard. "You think?" someone asked.

"Anyone would think," we said. "Don't call someone here who tries to tell you something different."

From Joe

"Ignorance is bliss." How true. And how relevant for a church with an endowment. First Christian Church of Odessa had a healthy endowment, bequests from a prior generation. But the biggest danger from the blessing of a permanent endowment fund is its capacity to keep the church ignorant of the true costs (and opportunities) of its ministry. The congregation was reliant on its endowment, spending it down at an alarming rate. Twenty percent of the operating budget was being underwritten by accumulated assets. The net result was that even the church's leadership had no reliable sense of the cost of ministry, or the capacity to evaluate its success. And despite that ignorance, they still did not enjoy enough bliss. Financially, each annual budgeting cycle induced misery. Our active membership was shrinking, and so were our annual pledged offerings.

When we first saw the downtown buildings, it was obvious that the congregation had an aging and impractical facility. The larger sanctuary building was built for a traffic flow and attendance level they hadn't seen in decades. The education and fellowship spaces were from a different time—narrow halls, stairs with no elevator, and traffic patterns no one would've designed today.

Later, when we became their pastors, we discovered the church also was the proud owner of an old-school, broken-down boiler heating system, patched back together time and time again. And we had other obsolete building systems that were costly to maintain. The common trope for aging and shrinking congregations is that they are left with a costly physical plant draining their resources. At times, the same is also true for payroll. Some churches have shrunk at the same rate as ours and found it difficult, impossible even, to reduce staff appropriately, especially when they had an endowment to use as a crutch. Fortunately for us, this was not the case. When we came on board, the church had the equivalent of three full-time employees.

When we held beginning conversations with church leadership about the possibility of big change, Dawn and I were quick to identify the financial obstacles of moving, of buying land, and of constructing or buying a new facility. Yet we also pointed out the costs of "doing nothing" or "doing only small things." The church's property expenses (insurance, utilities, maintenance, etc.) were twenty percent of our operating budget. That means we were spending down our endowment to keep us in a building that had become a hindrance to, rather than an enabler of, the ministry we sought to share in our community. The endowment served as a salve numbing us from the sting of reality.

Before we left town, the search committee told us they wanted us to be their pastors. They gave us a contract to consider. It was time to decide if we were going to uproot our lives. When we returned home, we had a houseguest, a family member recovering from surgery. We also had two children ages eleven and twelve. It was difficult to have a simple conversation at our house, much less to find space to decide if we were making a major life change.

So, Joe and I went on a drive. Where could we talk together in our small suburb, where over the past decade, we'd gotten to know just about everybody? No, not the coffee shop, not the Chinese restaurant, not the sandwich shop. Which is how we found ourselves finally rolling into the parking lot of our local funeral home. We had buried over 225 beloved people in our decade serving that congregation. The funeral home was like a second office to us. We pulled into the back parking lot, turned off the car, and looked each other in the eye. Taking a deep breath, we let the silence settle around us. Then, we began to talk.

It was a risk to go. We were concerned that the Odessa church was so small. If we couldn't help them turn around, we shouldn't stay more than three years, or we would just be adding to their plight. Were we too late in their decline to be of real help? We sure hated to uproot our kids for something so uncertain. It felt really risky, like a parachute jump for a family of four.

On the plus side, since college, I had harbored the burning hope of starting a new church. If we could somehow relaunch this church, I would get to do what I'd someday hoped to do. Joe always said if there was some financial stability for our children, we could start a new church. This seemed like the closest we would get. We loved the people. Our parents were in Texas. And, most of all, we felt needed, like our gifts were the right match for this congregation. When we took another deep breath, we could hear the faint whisper of a calling from God. So, we grabbed hands, and right there in the funeral home parking lot, we swung our hands three times and decided to jump.

We wrote a letter to go along with our acceptance. The letter said, in essence: please don't call us unless you are willing to consider relocating, because that is where we think we will lead. The search committee combined our letter with their own comments. They made it clear, writing to the congregation that "a vote to call this couple is a commitment to taking steps to relocate." The church voted almost unanimously to call us (except for one guy who wanted to know if we would preach against homosexuality, and we had already told the search committee we didn't think you needed to pray the gay away). And so, we broke our children's little hearts, paid way too much for a house in Odessa during an oil boom, and packed up for Texas.

More than once I wondered, *are we crazy?* Our first Sunday leading worship in Odessa, I really worried. Only about forty-five people came to worship that day. It was summertime still, I told myself. Actually, it was the second Sunday of September. Going from preaching for 325 people across three services to 45 people across two services seemed like a bad career move for a minute. Everyone was wonderfully welcoming, but still, the critical mass was not there. I wondered again if we were too late to make any significant difference. Not to mention that by November the oil boom was going bust. What had we done?

In Their Words **by John Gillian**

The Gillian/Williams families have been members of First Christian/Connection Christian Church for four generations. Leslie and I were married in the downtown location and our son was baptized there. Our roots in this congregation are deep. We cannot imagine belonging to any other church in Odessa.

During many family gatherings well before our congregation called Pastors Dawn and Joe, Leslie and I spoke about the need to relocate our church in order to grow and thrive in our community, often to the dismay of some of our extended family members. We observed the shrinking numbers attending our church activities, the lack of new faces in our services, and the deteriorating buildings downtown, and we realized that, although our church was and is financially sound, without dynamic leadership and continual growth, First Christian Church would not survive in any meaningful way.

Leslie and I both took on leadership roles when opportunities seemed right. The most consequential role for me was accepting a position on the pastoral search committee. When the Weakses came to Odessa the first time, they were given a complete tour of the church buildings and the community. During a dinner meeting, I remember Joe commenting, "If you just want pastors who will keep things the same, or if you just want another Baptist church, we are *not* the right pastors." It was at that moment that I knew, beyond any doubt, that we had invited the right people to guide us into the future.

CHAPTER 3

Church in Weird Places

Joe and I began by honoring the congregation as it was, in all its earnestness to be a faithful church. We knew that big change was coming, but it could not happen overnight. We leapt into the church's unique traditions, like Smorgasbord, an Advent gathering where the only foods allowed are finger foods. Smorgasbord requires a certain table configuration and very clean hands to pick up the deviled eggs, tiny sandwiches, and delicate cookies displayed in grand fashion. We also embraced Spaghetti Day, a sixty-five-year-old tradition that raises money for various local charities, and involves a secret recipe for the pasta sauce and somehow serving coleslaw on the plate as a side. The real key to success, however, is all the homemade desserts sliced up and added to sweeten the deal. (The most recent Spaghetti Day raised $5000 for our local domestic violence shelter.) Joe and I were determined to appreciate all the congregation's traditions. We came to love all the characters in the congregation, too.

There was Richard, the World War II veteran; Marilyn, whose voice makes her seem gruff but who has a heart of gold; and Les, the retired Marine who wore his cookie monster pajamas to our Christmas pajama party. Not to mention Marthana, the elderly tap dancer, and Oralee who calls the church office a few times a month just to let us know she loves us. We also met our downtown neighbors, all small businesses in the surrounding area. We did prayer walks through the streets around the church to get a feel for who and what was there. And we started tending to the homeless camp that had built up by the church garage.

Pastor Joe became the landlord. He learned names and made rules: You have to be dressed by 9:00 a.m.; you can use the church hose, but only in a certain place; no smoking, no fighting, and no drugs. A parade of personalities came through our little patio. I remember Smoky, a young, slender man who didn't talk much, but who helped us with yard work from time to time. One Christmas Eve, Smoky helped me set out luminarias to line our sidewalks with light. The next Christmas Eve, he was back in jail, and we were sending a Christmas card to him. The homeless camp may seem like a small detail, but it was the kind of thing that helped our church reconnect to our community.

Our church held a forum for all the organizations that work with the displaced. We also drew in our campers for worship sometimes. We were desperate for more people to share God's love with, no matter their housing status. It seemed God was working on our hearts, asking, "Are you desperate enough to let me work through you? And if I come to you in the face of an unexpected, unkempt person, will you see me in their desperation?"

From Joe

"It's not about us." Our long preparation for the discernment process focused on intentionality of purpose. Why is our church here? And the answer was inevitably that we exist as a faith community not only for those of us in the church, but for the sake of God's children outside the walls.

One small circumstance that moved our congregation was the homeless camp that developed on our property. Downtown unhoused folks started camping under the porch outside our garage. Being in conversation with them, it quickly became clear that running them off simply meant putting them on someone else's porch. So, we decided to work with them. Nobody *wanted* homeless people on our property. One Sunday morning, an older church lady who always came in from the back walked past a man changing his shirt! It caused quite a stir. But being in relationship with and working with those folks postured us to act not based on what made us comfortable, but as a church following Jesus. As small as our ministry was, it challenged our sense of who we are and why we exist.

Many years ago, I was in an annual training for elders. A new elder asked, "Do we pick up the bread tray and hand it to the deacon, and then pick up the cup tray and hand it over? Or do we pick them both up at the same time, and hand them over both at once?" A senior elder blurted out, "No, we hand the bread and cup at the same time. I like it that way." I thought to myself: actually, Jesus passed one and then the other. I've never forgotten my disappointment at an elder using the criteria "I like it that way" as a standard for how we conduct our ministry. We will not be faithful to Christ's ministry if our criteria are what we like and what makes us comfortable.

A daycare was another connection to our community. Two women who ran a trusted daycare in the area outgrew their space and were looking for a new place to host their kiddos. It meant putting fire sprinklers in our education building, which was an expensive chore, but it also meant sixty small people would be running around our building, filling it with more energy than it had known in a very long time. Our church leadership jumped on the opportunity. They did so not because it would bring in new families to join our church but because they were saying "yes" to opportunities whenever they could. I'd worked at churches with daycares. I warned our leadership that rarely do families want their kids to spend all week somewhere and then bring them back on Sundays. We welcomed these children, not because of what it would do for us, but because we felt God calling us to open the doors and let the children come in. We wanted more life in our buildings. We brought those babies through our doors, and our building began to sound like a church building should, with children's laughter in the hallways. Our congregation began to feel the breeze blow through our open windows. We were practicing saying yes to God even if we didn't know what that meant, exactly. The Holy Spirit was working in us.

The more reconnected the church became to the community, the more Joe and I learned about the corporate memory of our church. Our congregation's roots as a leader in the community were over a hundred years old. We were one of the first four churches established in Odessa. We helped start Meals on Wheels and Habitat for Humanity in our town. We established a low-income housing apartment complex for the elderly. For decades, we were at the forefront of ecumenical efforts to alleviate poverty, racism, and sexism, and to advance educational opportunities. We had a long history of making a difference for the down and out. In a previous place I had served, I had been occasionally reminded by church leadership of expectations about how many hours I should spend in the office. But at First Christian Church of Odessa, folks took great joy when they heard about what Joe and I were doing out in the community. They didn't expect us to be behind a desk in an office. They wanted us to be wherever the community was hurting. Those were our church's roots, and they weren't as dormant as they seemed.

Joe and I both joined a program called Leadership Odessa that helped catapult our church even further into community involvement. Most cities offer this type of leadership program through their Chamber of Commerce. They may not all have these kinds of results. But the pioneer mentality of our town always has been that if you came here to help, grab a shovel. Leadership Odessa immediately introduced us to people and places who needed help when it would've taken us years to find them on our own. Through Leadership Odessa, both Joe and I spent time giving one Thursday a month to tour our town, meet the people who make it happen, and learn about what the community needs and where it shines. We visited the hospitals, the food bank, a manufacturing plant, our university, the community theatre, and everything in between.

Leadership Odessa led us to do our own quest. Over the course of our first year in Odessa, I met with leaders from every outreach organization the church had supported in recent years. I also talked to local education leaders, law enforcement, health professionals, and many others. I wanted to get "it" before we decided where our place in "it" was. Sometimes church growth consultants challenge churches to think about the question, "If your church closed its doors today, who would miss you?" The question is intended to help you discern if your congregation is making any impact in the community it inhabits. We at the very least were determined to be missed!

So, before our church was even ready to move, we developed a community coalition where we could both be a blessing and receive blessings untold. We identified places where the support of Christian community was desperately needed but mostly absent—places like the juvenile detention center, the domestic violence shelter, and even our school district. We wanted to be where our neighbors hurt the most and had the least help. We looked for places where we could deeply invest over the long haul, to prove ourselves worthy of trust and to show that we were not just people looking for a quick-fix service project. We wanted to find out where the church was already missed and set up shop there.

Our first really big step outside of our walls was La Promesa, a public housing apartment complex about two miles from the church. Because of my experiences in our Kansas City church, one of my community-related questions was, "How do poor kids get food for the summer when they don't get it from school lunch programs?" Turns out Odessa kids needed to go to a school somewhat near them during summer school, which ran through June. After that, nothing was planned beyond families accessing local food pantries. This unmet need called out to our church. After talking with the West Texas Food Bank leadership, we identified La Promesa as a place where we could serve lunch from Kids Cafe, a federal program. The food would be provided; we just had to serve it and supervise the kids while they ate.

Our sixth summer now has passed feeding kids, Monday through Friday, all summer long. From this deep connection, we developed a tutoring ministry for the kids during the school year. We now partner with our local art museum to provide kids with art classes as well. We have walked alongside several individual families in multiple ways. We've been blessed by kids who graduated high school and went off to college, and we've been heartbroken by some we've seen drop out and live lives of addiction and crime. We've held funerals for friends there, and helped single parents find access to childcare and jobs. One thing has been obvious: *church happens at La Promesa, even though we're not at church.*

That truth has been an essential learning for us: church can happen in weird places. If we were to move beyond the stuck place where the church had been existing, we had to figure out how to do and be church without the building. We needed to be so eager to share and experience God's love in Jesus Christ that it didn't matter where it happened, as long as it happened. Getting out of the box of traditional church was becoming our new habit.

Enter "Ashes to Go." A nationwide movement, Ashes to Go is about taking the normally highly liturgical imposition of ashes on Ash

Wednesday out to street corners and coffee shops so that it meets people where they are.[3] We began bringing this sacred practice to gas stations, grocery stores, coffee shops, our hospitals, and the street corner by our church building, offering ashes and prayer. This opened our eyes very quickly to how many Christians are without a church home in our community, and how many people are willing to have a stranger pray with them. People come easily; it takes no arm-twisting. "Would you like ashes and a prayer?" we ask. About half of people walk away, and about half say yes. This event is regularly noted in our local newspaper and TV stations as well. We create press releases and get wonderful coverage, even in surrounding towns. And all we are doing is taking church outside of its walls to people who need it. Now in our sixth year of Ashes to Go, we have people who are our regulars, who for whatever reason can't or don't go to church but think of us as their church. Sometimes they even give an offering when they come to get their ashes. This is a start in their connection with Jesus, and we are grateful.

Not long ago, I gave the invocation for a Salvation Army fundraising banquet at a nice hotel in town. A middle-aged, short, soft-spoken man gave a testimony. I could have sworn I'd never seen him before in my life, but he pointed to me and said, "You don't remember me, do you? One day I was sleeping on the fire escape of your church building. You woke me up. You explained that a daycare met upstairs in your church, and you had to keep the stairs free for them. Then you handed me a coffee. It was the most conversation I'd had in weeks." I remembered, but I wouldn't have recognized him all cleaned up. He had an apartment and a job and some hope, so he looked like a new man.

When you seek Jesus for real, when you really want to do what he would have you do, it begins to change everything. Our community connections, where we sought to bless others, began to bless us. People in town started to know who our church was again, and not because we took out an ad on TV, though we did that later. Word of mouth was that the old Christian church truly wanted to show you how much God loves you—whoever and wherever you are. They would do anything, anywhere.

---

[3] https://ashestogo.org

Once people of faith remember that church doesn't have to happen at church, well, anything and anywhere is possible. We had church at Homemade Wines, a neighborhood wine bar, by starting a Bible study there. We held Bible studies at Chick-fil-A, law offices, and grocery stores. We had church around tables at Zucchi's restaurant, as a "dinner church" model. We had church at a park where we offered potluck to the whole neighborhood. We had church at the Blanton Elementary cafetorium, for fifteen months, God help us. By the time we moved into a more permanent location, we knew that church wasn't a building. Not at all. And thank God for that, because when the pandemic hit and we started doing church in a parking lot, it didn't seem like a big deal to do church in weird places anymore.

In Their Words by Reneé Earls

Upon moving back home after college more than three decades ago, I was searching for a new church home. I knew it would feel right for me when I found a place to grow spiritually. After many visits to various churches of different denominations, I jumped in at First Christian Church, now known as Connection Christian Church. The reasons were many, but the immense community outreach was certainly one of the most appealing to me.

The mentality of the church going beyond the walls of the main facility goes back more than 100 years for our congregation. From the onset of the church's creation in 1906, the members have been immersed in community projects. The long-standing Spaghetti Dinner is one example. For more than six decades, this large event has attracted hundreds of eaters who help fund a special outreach project. Availability of affordable housing in our area is a continually difficult issue, so in the 1990s, our congregation founded Disciples Village, a low-income senior housing facility. That ministry remains vital in our effort to connect with seniors to meet their needs. On the opposite of the age spectrum, our members serve as mentors to young people at the Ector County Youth Center, giving those students hope in a time of despair. A tutoring ministry not only encourages school children in their classwork, but also connects multiple generations, encouraging life-changing relationships.

These few examples of outreach are simply a snapshot of our love and compassion for our community. When there is a need for a spiritual component in any local project, the community thinks of Connection Christian Church. Our church's name is synonymous with outreach and community. In Matthew 22:39, Jesus says, "Love your neighbor as yourself." We take that part of the Bible literally at Connection Christian Church.

CHAPTER 4

Fearless

It took three years to see real transformation happen. Three years, and I was forced to finally shed the layer of people-pleasing I'd worn throughout my whole ministry. For too long I struggled, if someone gave me a cross look or quit coming to worship, to move ahead with confidence.

Over my years of ministry, I have endured some highly critical people. Turns out I had developed fears I didn't realize were bogging me down until I was serving as a pastor in this new place. The first time we decorated the downtown church buildings for the Advent season, I was paralyzed with fear that I would displease someone. The decorating team gathered, and when they began putting silk poinsettias in place, I felt my stomach tighten.

Before we arrived as their pastors, the congregation had moved worship out of the big sanctuary because it was too vacuous for the current number of people who came. The sanctuary didn't have a functional air conditioner or heater, nor did the baptistry work. So, they converted the gymnasium back into the worship space it had once been in the 1940s. Our first year there was their first time decorating this new-from-the-old space for Advent. Nothing had its place yet. Still everyone, it seemed, wanted to use the same decorations that they'd used for decades in the old sanctuary, including eighty-five-year-old Joyce, a strong-willed, dedicated saint of the church. She wanted to use the old nativity set, even though it was too large to go on the now-smaller chancel. I worried. What right did I have to buck her? Couldn't we just walk around the towering figures?

The amount of emotional energy I put into where the decorations should go on our first Advent together, trying so hard not to hurt anyone's feelings, was disproportionate to how much it all mattered. In fact, I recently asked Joyce what she remembers about our decorating dilemmas seven years ago. Yes, at ninety-two years old, she is still very active in our congregation. She said she thought our first time decorating together went just fine. "No biggie!" she said. My anxiety revealed how trained I was to try to smooth over the difficulties of how we all feel about change. The gnawing pit of fear in my spirit had to be met with some healing balm if we were going to see God transform this congregation in far bigger ways than the placement of Christmas decorations.

Our theme for 2015 became "Fearless." It worked out that it was also the theme of the local favorite Texas Tech football team that year, so the church easily adopted "Fearless" as its own motto. Some church members gave me "Fearless" perfume and I found a bracelet that said "Fearless" which I wore nearly every day for a year. I determined to fake it till I made it. Joe and I preached about people who made fearless choices in the Bible. For our "Fearless" process, we partnered with Hope Partnership through the Christian Church (Disciples of Christ). Rick Morse, a denominational leader, helped us through a congregational study and discussion about relocating. We had four small groups that met six times each, looking at the demographics in our church and community, studying scripture, praying, and talking about what they hoped for our church.

Though our goal was to be fearless, it wasn't to be aloof. Through our process of discussing relocation possibilities, we wanted to be very much in touch with everyone who cared about our church. Our hope was to include the whole congregation, to make everyone feel heard, and to help everybody to feel like their perspective mattered. All along, Joe and I said that we wanted the process to be so inclusive and thorough that at the end of it, everyone would say, "I thought we already decided this. Why are we voting?" The congregational process gave us that level of engagement.

But it did not give us a direction. At the end of it, Joe and I sat down with the leaders of the small groups. Each leader shared the overarching desires of their group for the church. As we went around the circle sharing, my spirits dropped. It became clear our leaders had reached a stalemate. While we had been given options for the future of the church through the process we used, there was no clear consensus from the groups. Two groups wanted to move elsewhere, and two groups wanted to stay and try harder. How could we please everybody? If that was our goal, we were doomed to fail. We could not make consensus our aim. We did a lot of work to be in touch with all of our congregation. Now we needed to be in touch with God.

From Joe

"The tyranny of the minority." In a society or a congregation where we act based on majority vote, one would think that the will of the majority is the basis of what we do. However, social psychology and identity theory describe how it often works in the real world—the tyranny of the minority. No matter how clear a decision, there will always be the potential for a percentage of folks to vote "no" or "yes." This becomes a problem when a minority opinion becomes an excuse for not acting. It can play out in the church as "I'd like to vote yes, but I don't want to upset these folks." This occurs often because of the passion of the minority, as compared to that of the majority. It turns out that if we only move on possibilities that everyone agrees on, then we won't move. The goal is not 100%.

When we voted to move, 93% of our folks voted yes to selling our building, and 87% voted yes on the new location our team had picked out. That is a crazy high percentage. Had it been 70%, we would've still gone forward straight away.

It was time for a gut check. At this point we were nearly two years into the work. Personally, I was struggling because we had pulled our kids out of a church with a vibrant children and youth ministry, yet still we were far from that happening for them in our current situation. Joe and I were hoping the transformation would happen faster. And hadn't we sent a letter to the congregation saying, "This is what we need to do, so don't call us if you're not ready?" We breathed deeply and tried to remind ourselves to trust and not be afraid.

During this time, "Fearless" became my mantra for a whole different reason. Out of the blue, and with no family history, I was diagnosed with breast cancer following my annual mammogram. We caught it early. Still, it was the big "C" and I cried more than a few tears. The next months were a blur of doctor appointments and various scans.

When I went in for my CAT scan with my belly and veins full of barium, the room was freezing cold. The hospital gown, uh, didn't help. My teeth were chattering. Christine, the radiology technician, put a warm cotton blanket over me as I went into the machine. I remembered Genesis chapter 3 where God sews clothes for Adam and Eve. You remember that one? They have to move out of Eden into the world's brokenness. And they don't want to be naked out there. They are dressed with clothes our seamstress God made by her own hands.

This is what it was like when I told the congregation I had breast cancer. Over the coldness of cancer, they wrapped the warmth of their prayers and care for me, for Joe, and for the kids. Sometimes I wonder if we were able to go through the hard thing of relocating the church together at least in part because our congregation went through this cancer valley with us. We came out with a stronger relationship between pastors and people, and with the renewed assurance that God wasn't finished with any of us yet.

My lumpectomy was on a Friday morning. Amy, the search committee member who had first called to ask us to consider coming to Odessa, prayed over me before I went back for surgery. A cadre of church ladies kept Joe company while he waited for the good report: no cancer in the lymph nodes. It had not spread! I showed up for church that Sunday, 48 hours after surgery. I was weak, but able. I didn't lead in worship. In fact, it was difficult to even stand and sing. But I wanted to be there, to soak in the congregation's love, and to encourage them that I was going to be okay. That morning, one of our elders privately presented me with a prayer shawl her sister had made for me. She placed it lightly on my shoulders while she and her young daughter offered a prayer for me. I knew I would be alright, and I am.

A few months later, the church board gathered to hear the inconclusive reports from our long study process. It was disheartening. We listened to every angle presented. We were at a dead end if we were trying to be in touch with doing what the congregation wanted to do. We prayed, we discussed, we scratched our heads. No clear direction emerged.

Then Bill Davis spoke up. Bill is a soft-spoken, retired construction supervisor who is a widower and a churchman. He loves Jesus, so much that he was our property chair at the time. It takes a special kind of saint to be a church property chair. Bill knew more than anyone how much energy and money the upkeep of our current buildings sapped from us. He took a breath and cleared his throat. And when Bill talks, people listen. All eyes turned to him. Then he firmly yet gently said, "This is why we are here. Our congregation appointed us to lead, and we need to lead. Don't think any more about what people want us to do. We need to think about what God wants us to do."

As soon as Bill spoke, the tension in the room released. Our consternation shifted to a buzz of anticipation. "That's right," someone said. "Yes, I agree," another piped up. Before we knew it, the board had developed a recommendation to the congregation that we put our property on the market and begin exploring a purchase of new property. Decisions to accept a contract on the old building or issue a contract on a new location would still be voted upon by the congregation in next steps. The board was not deciding, but it was leading.

We developed three teams: Launching, Landing, and Mission. Launching would research selling our property and what to do with all of our stuff. Landing would research both temporary and permanent new homes. And Mission would prayerfully discern our "why" about how a move would help us reach our community, and develop the marketing, evangelism, and outreach plan to do it. Two weeks later, in a called congregational meeting, the congregation voted overwhelmingly (though not unanimously) to explore the possibilities...and we were off!

In Their Words by Bill Davis

I was really surprised when the Weakses said they would come to Odessa. When they did, they told the whole congregation in a letter that we needed to be ready to relocate because that's where they would lead us. I read that letter, and everyone in the congregation who voted to bring them here should have read it. They were very clear.

But two years after they came, we were still discussing change instead of acting on it. I was frustrated. In that board meeting, it just seemed like nobody wanted to step up and say anything that would move us along. I guess I can understand—a lot of them had been in the church for years and years. It's where they had gotten married and had funerals. I didn't have that long of a history with the church. It just upset me that everyone was waiting on someone else to say something. So, I did. I simply said that our pastors told us this was where we were headed two years prior, and now it was time for us to lead with them. Everything started to move in the right direction after that meeting.

Looking back, I believe there's no question we did the right thing. Even the deniers at that time will now say 100% that our move was needed. If you've never gone through this big of a change, it's hard to realize what all we've been through—packing up, meeting in a school cafeteria, and getting our new building ready. We even had a water pipe that burst two days before our grand opening that baptized half the place. This is not to mention the 2021 Texas freeze and this whole COVID-19 pandemic. But we are still going strong, with lots of new people in our church, and still getting guests all the time. That would not have happened if we had not moved. We absolutely did the right thing, and God has blessed it.

CHAPTER 5

The Requirement for Resurrection

When the church building went on the market, it caused a stir. We created a sign to go above the "For Sale" sign so we could steer the narrative a little. Our sign proclaimed "We're On the Move" and had our website address so people could get the bigger story. Those signs were a shock to the system. Our church office fielded a few phone calls from long-lost members decrying the change in the church. It seemed folks who hadn't sent a dollar or darkened the door of our church for years had strong opinions about what we should be doing. As a former pastor of of a few churches, I understood. They had invested a lot a long time ago, and still wanted to see things go a certain way. But thankfully the movie *Frozen* had recently been released, and anyone who answered the phone was encouraged to "let it go" in their hearts as they listened to well-intentioned but no-current-investment concerns.

We were releasing our church buildings into God's hands and waiting to see what would happen. Meanwhile, all we could do was wait and pray. We wondered if our neighbor church would be interested in buying. For years, a light-hearted and sometimes not-so-lighthearted feud had smoldered between our church and the Baptist church next door. We shared a parking lot for decades, with our now-small church on the south side of the lot, and their now-big church on the north side where a major intersection was. Their congregants would park in the spaces allocated to our church. It didn't matter that we might not need those spaces—they were our spaces! Someone bought big, bright orange traffic cones and wrote "First Christian Church" on the side. Every Sunday our custodian would haul those cones out and mark "our" spaces. The effort became futile as their church grew and started providing traffic shuttles on golf carts, while we struggled to fill the spaces we had. Our church was becoming dwarfed by the overreaching neighbor.

Once, a couple accidentally came to worship at our downtown church, intending to go to the church next door. As they were hastily leaving after the service was over, I rushed out to greet them. "We're so glad you came!" I gushed. "What brought you today?" The man hesitated but the woman told it like it was. "We meant to visit the Baptist church. We just didn't want to be rude and leave when we realized we were in the wrong place. This church is dead!"

Well, we weren't dead. Perhaps we had just been switched to life support? But wow, was that an affirmation that exploring a relocation was the way to go. Maybe God was up to some resurrection work. After all, don't you have to be pronounced dead to be properly resurrected?

We had a hunch our Baptist neighbors would want to buy our buildings, even if just for the parking lot. After a daycare, a funeral home, and another church looked at it, our neighbors came through and offered to buy our buildings for $1.45 million. Some in our congregation thought we would get more money for the buildings, but real estate appraisals made it clear that this was a fair price. We were all relieved the buildings would remain useful to a church, even if it was to take over our parking lot! We gave thanks to God for divine provision. After closing, we leased the building back from the Baptists for a few months until we could get our own arrangements in order.

And that was a big challenge! Figuring out where to go was complicated. Of course, the first dream was to find an ideally located plot of land, build on it, and expect that "they would come." You know, like the church of the 1950s? But that was a no-go. Our region was experiencing another oil boom, and land was so pricey it would have taken all of our money to buy property. What we would have been able to build if we had purchased land would have been pretty paltry. We looked into temporary "sprung" buildings we could live in for five to ten years until we could raise the money to put a building on our expensive land. Some thought surely someone would donate land to us because our church had historic ties to folks with land, but that did not happen. We had endowment money we could have used, but we did not want to cough it all up in one fell swoop. And, in addition to depleting the endowment, we still would have had to pivot all of our energy to fundraising. Buying land was a non-starter. Yet the prospects of buying an existing building seemed depressing at first.

From Joe

"If you place your trust in God, God will provide." "Good stewardship means spending within your means." "You've got to spend money to make money." The problem with great wisdom is that it often conflicts with other great wisdom.

As a church in discernment, the practical, financial side of the equation was important. We wanted to dream big dreams, but we did not want to cripple the congregation and its mission with big debt. Capital expansion and growth means raising capital funds, through some combination of investors and debt, in the business world as well as in church growth. Deciding to move meant deciding to spend down our endowment, and to launch a capital campaign to assess how much money was available to invest in a new location.

Part of our decision *to* move was based on our assessment that we *could* afford to move in a sustainable way. We focused on the equity we had—building value, capital donor payables, and cash on hand. We did not want to land in a location with $1 million+ debt that was left to the next generation of church folk to pay. But we were also aware that the sustainability mark was a moving target; we were taking a risk.

We looked at buildings on the market that we identified as promising, trying to keep an open mind. We endeavored to think big, beyond just church buildings, so that God could surprise us with what might be possible. We were inspired by the story of a sister church, First Christian in Bentonville, Arkansas. They were launching a satellite location and discovered a large barn for sale in the right area for their ministry. But the pastor told his wife, "I am not worshipping in a barn." She quickly answered back, "Well, if it was good enough for Jesus..." Now, Waterway Christian Church thrives in that beautifully renovated barn! With that inspiration, we drew our circle widely. We looked at office buildings, movie theatres, and even a honkytonk that was for sale. We would have looked at a barn had one been available. After all, if it was good enough for Jesus....

The buildings all blur together for me, but one stood out as a klunker: a 1970's-era semi-abandoned church poised just off of the growing part of town. Our "Landing" team dutifully traipsed around every part of the odd property. This dusty little church had a run-down, small, octagonal sanctuary, which would've been pretty cool to worship in, actually. But quirkiest of all, this property had a prayer tower, a la Oral Roberts. You could climb up in that thing and look over a large part of the city and pray for it. Or whatever else people do in prayer towers that are open to the public. It was pretty rank in there, filled with bugs, trash, and broken beer bottles. We were hard pressed to find much fodder for prayer. This gem even came with a double-wide trailer house next door, where the founding pastor and his family had once lived. Maybe Joe and I could move to the church?!

Thank goodness that was a "no." It would have taken a lot of work—and fumigation—to make that location a workable solution. It was also a little far out from a population center, with no guarantee growth would come its way. But the imagination that our people tried to have about that strange spot was great training. *We learned to look at places with an eye, not for what was there, but for what it could be.* That's how we found our dream corner at Tanglewood Lane and Penbrook Street. Pastor Joe drove by this empty medical office building on a highly visible corner one day and thought, *that's perfect, except it needs a raised roof for a sanctuary and it's way too big for us. But, let's look.*

A builder named Chuck Sturgeon met our "Landing" task force at the potential site. A successful engineer with his own building company, Chuck is also a devout Catholic who thanks God for his success by helping churches at cost. Without Chuck and his team, I doubt we would have had the gumption to make the leap. That's what it was like, living into this adventure. Our leaders just kept stepping, one step at a time, not being sure that our next step had a place to land, but stepping out anyway. "For we walk by trust, not by sight," 2 Corinthians 5:7 says. We were living that every day, and every day God was showing us tangible reasons to keep trusting, through people like Chuck.

Chuck kicked around in the building with us. We walked through the pediatrician's office and the dialysis lab. We each stood on the wheelchair scale and jumped off before the rest of the group could see our weight numbers. We looked at the huge x-ray machine in one of the office suites and wondered how it could be reused for gospel purposes?!? It was hard to imagine this as a church, and yet…. Chuck said, "We can raise the roof on this thing, if you want it."

Did we want it? It was huge—30,000 square feet, the same size as our downtown building which we were only using half of, at best. It seemed dumb to buy another building that was oversized for us. But we wondered…what about sharing it? The rent costs in our city are always astronomical because of the oil field influence, which is hard on nonprofits. What if we developed the office space into a "shared spaces" kind of concept? Would people get on board?

It needs to be said that our church held an advantage over a brand-new church start. We were a somewhat-known entity in the community. True, we were a shadow of what we had been once, but people who remembered us held long trust for First Christian Church of Odessa. Our church had been one of the first four churches in the community, along with the Baptists, Presbyterians, and Methodists. When you hear me say we were starting anew, it wasn't without roots. Our prayer was to take the healthy DNA of what our congregation started out to be and transplant that into fertile ground. Gina Yarbrough, our church historian, found a newspaper clipping from the 1940s that celebrated the opening of the first sanctuary at our old location. The headline read: "Progressive, Cooperative, Friendly." That's who we were in 1948. Could we be that anew seventy years later in 2017? To find out, we emailed out a survey to leaders of all of the nonprofit organizations in Odessa. We asked if they might consider officing out of our potential new church building. Enough people were interested that we were assured it wasn't a crazy idea to host nonprofits in our excess space.

From Joe

"Use it or lose it." Churches for many, many years have lamented that even in the most vibrant faith communities, the church building mostly goes empty and unused during the week. We looked at many options when deciding where to land. Should we build? Should we buy a church? Should we buy a commercial building and renovate it into a church? We landed on the latter. It is fun to say our fellowship community hall used to be a dialysis center. One factor of our search was an idea, a dream. When laying the groundwork to think outside ourselves, we became even more involved with the great work that nonprofits do in our community. One of our hopes became to find a facility that would allow us to partner with and support some of those nonprofits in an official capacity. We found a building with extra office space and christened the north section of the building the "Connection Center." And the organizations came. We filled up immediately. Some moved in before we did. They pay a monthly lease that is well below market and are thrilled to do so. We are delighted they are here, and their lease underwrites three-fourths of our property costs, including staff.

Our Catholic contractor who was willing to work for us at cost posed a question: Are you ready to raise the roof on this 1980s medical building? Time to make more decisions. Our Landing team met and talked about the great location of this building, the work that would be ahead, and whether or not we really could get some nonprofits to partner with us. Nothing was certain, but the excitement for what might be possible was growing. After about two hours of conversation, David Yarbrough, a leader of the church for thirty years, said, very matter-of-factly, "I think we should do it." His decisiveness was contagious, and we determined to recommend this building to our congregation.

Getting this empty 1980s medical building back on line, much less transformed to become a church and nonprofit center, was a daunting task. Thankfully one of our church leaders, Bryan Paddack, is an engineer. Bryan drew an architectural rendering of what the building could look like, with a raised roof in the middle for a sanctuary. He even included a place for the bell tower that people knew and loved from our downtown location. When Bryan took our hopes and made them tangible, using his skill to put imagination to paper, our congregation's uncertainty grew into excitement. Bryan's drawing gave us the clear vision we needed. We blew that image up really big, put it on a poster in our worship space, and started to plan. The building was listed for $2.2 million, but because we are a church, the owner offered to sell it to us for $1.5 million. It had been her medical doctor husband's office building. She wanted to see it used again for healing in our community. She didn't know that $1.5 million was basically what we had been offered for our old building. But God did!

On Easter Sunday, 2017, we celebrated Christ's victory over death and pronounced that God was doing a resurrection work in our church too. That very next Sunday, our congregation met after worship to decide if we should sell and buy. If you have bought and sold property, you know this is not how it normally happens. You don't usually get to see properties move in synchronized conjunction with each other. Not only did we both have an offer on our buildings and a contract to make an offer on a new building, but the two amounts were within $50,000 of each other! That Eastertide Sunday, our congregation voted both to sell our current buildings for $1.45 million and to buy our new-to-us facility for $1.5 million. Yes, the same day, and almost exactly the same amount. And that is how we knew, beyond a shadow of a doubt, that God still cared about our church and had plans for our future.

A few weeks after the church voted to take this leap of faith, we held a groundbreaking ceremony to ask for the Lord's help in our new building endeavor. With about seventy-five folks, including members of our congregation and supporters from the community, we prayed over this medical office building, that it would become holy ground. Representatives from the church from ages 9 to 92 each turned a spade of dirt to symbolically begin its transformation. Evanell Truskowski, one of the first women architects in Texas and a member of our congregation, got her son to bring her out to the groundbreaking in her wheelchair. She was eager to see her beautiful downtown historic church become a more modern, accessible congregation in a new location. She was not going to miss it. After the ceremony, I asked, "What do you think, Evanell?" She had two words for me: "Let's go!"

Go we did, but there were obstacles to overcome. The city wanted us to put fire sprinklers throughout this huge building. We could not move into the new building until it passed the city's inspection, and installing fire sprinklers increased our cost by $200,000 from the get-go. It also caused major labor delays because when the oil field is booming, workers who do this kind of skilled labor are hard to come by. It took nearly a year to get our sprinklers fully installed and inspected.

During that time, we could not be in the building for any reason. We worshiped in an elementary school (more on that later), moved our offices and youth group meetings to our home, and held Bible studies in various places. Meanwhile, the entire middle section of our new-to-us building was gutted. The roof was raised on that section and the building began to look a bit more like a church and less like an office building. Once the wall studs were in, our youth group got busy with Sharpie markers, writing scriptures, Christian symbols, and "fruit of the Spirit" words on each metal stud. It was starting to feel like a sacred space.

The external walls of our new building are "tilt wall" construction. Most thought they weren't very attractive. We discussed painting them but the maintenance on painting concrete, outdoor walls would be never-ending. What we *could* do was paint the new exterior walls we created by raising the roof over the sanctuary. The debate on what color to paint them seemed endless. A nice neutral color was the obvious choice. But one visionary in our group, an artist, suggested that we go with something bold, a color that would stand out in our retail area with lots of signage and buildings. We thought, *we haven't come this far to fade into the background now.* So, we went with a bright blue. If passersby had yet to notice our church rising up out of the former medical building, now they wouldn't be able to miss it.

We started holding church workdays every Saturday. Anyone with a little time to share came to paint, replace ceiling tiles, clear out old cabling, chip away adhesive on walls, or encourage and feed those who were working. One of our most faithful Saturday volunteers was Sarah Grove, a retired teacher in her eighties, and a beloved children's Sunday school leader for fifty-four years. Not 5.4 years; 54 years. Sarah needed a cane to walk, but she insisted on coming to work days nearly every Saturday. "If you'll just let me stay in one place, and get me a chair to sit in, I can paint," she'd say, and she nearly single-handedly repainted our children's ministry area. At least the bottom half of the walls was all Sarah! Lots of people put sweat equity in, and you could tell transformation was on its way.

In Their Words **by Sarah Grove**

I was against it! Move?! We've been here for over a hundred years! Change our name?! I've moved several times, but I didn't have to change my name! Not use my beloved denominational chalice as our logo?! This chalice is recognized worldwide as the symbol of the Christian Church (Disciples of Christ)! They wanted to take away everything I cared for!

No, not everything. Not the people, and they are the true church. I couldn't stand the thought of being somewhere else. I loved our pastors, and the leaders who were working so hard for this move were all people I'd known a long time and loved and trusted. So, I went to their meetings and planning sessions.

Suddenly our building was sold, and we had bought a big sprawling building that didn't look anything like a church. And we had moved worship into a school while the new building was being renovated. Yet, lo and behold, our "church" continued together and spread outside our walls and even grew in members. Over a year later, on Palm Sunday, we moved into our new sanctuary. What a celebration of joy and thanksgiving. And we could share our wonderful space with several nonprofits—an added blessing.

Then around the next Easter, the whole world shut down with the COVID-19 virus. We could no longer gather or hug, but our church did not shut down. Our worship services went virtual, we met for drive-in worship, and our community work continued to spread.

Now, we are gathering again in person, safely. What an exciting and wonderful journey this has been. God's blessings have poured over us and run out to all parts of Odessa. I am proud to be a part of that "blue building" called Connection Christian Church.

CHAPTER 6
A Blast from the Past

"First" is what churches were named a hundred years ago. If you were the first church of your denomination to reach the town you were in, you were thereby christened First Baptist, First Christian, First Presbyterian, First Methodist, and so on. That was the configuration of churches within a mile of each other in downtown Odessa, all developed at the turn of the twentieth century. It's amazing to me that for a religion in which the founder instructed his followers that "those who are last will be first, and those who are first will be last," the trend was "First" Church instead of "Last" Church.[4] This tells us something about the pioneer mentality, and how the first white people to claim the land got to name it. "Last" would have aged better.

By the twenty-first century, in our town, there were nine "First Something" churches. Not to mention all the "Firsts" in closely surrounding towns. This alone propelled our congregational leadership to think about changing our name. How were people supposed to find us or remember us when there were so many other churches that sounded similar? To further prompt us to consider a name change, the biggest of the First churches in town had recently rebranded to get rid of the "Baptist" in their name. They were now simply "First Odessa." To heck with the other eight First churches in Odessa, apparently. It reminded me of a grade school chant, "We're number one! We can't be number two! We're gonna beat the whoopee out of you!" Still, there were no "Last" churches in town, but I digress.

It was obvious that the conversation about changing our name needed to happen. Except I really, really, really did not want to do this. I had change fatigue. I was guessing the congregation had change fatigue.

---

[4] Matthew 20:16

I called up Rick Morse, who helped us navigate the early part of our transition process, and said, "Rick, do we have to make them think about this? Is the name that important?" And he said, "You will not give yourself the fresh start you are hoping for if you don't change your name. A new name won't guarantee a new future, but the old name will block it." Fine. We resigned to initiate the conversation.

First, Joe and I shared in a sermon series about name changes in scripture. From Jacob-to-Israel to Simon-to-Peter, the Bible celebrates name changes as evidence that God is at work in an individual or a community. Isaiah 62 celebrates that you were once called "Deserted" but will now be called "Desired."[5] We had once been "First" but now hoped to be "Servant." We had been "Dying" but hoped to become "Vibrantly Alive."

Our "Mission" task force took up the naming conversation. We began by leaning into scripture. The story of the feeding of the 5,000 in chapter 6 of Mark's gospel called to us. This story centered us in what the gospel is and who our congregation is within it. We made a list of church names that bubbled up from that story. Then we crossed off any that were already taken by churches in a thirty-mile radius. We didn't want to be in the "First" situation all over again. All of this took about six meetings and a lot of prayer over two months, always at the same table at Rosa's Café and Tortilla Factory.

That part in Mark chapter 6 about Jesus feeling "compassion over" the people because they were like sheep without a shepherd really got under our skin and into our hearts.[6] We kept coming back to how he cared about those who didn't have a guide. We all knew people like that; we had all been those people. To us, connection seemed like what people needed—both the people Jesus saw then, and those he saw now through our eyes. People, like sheep, needed connection to a guide, and connection with a flock to journey alongside. Someone suggested "Connection" as a name. It said a whole lot more about the heart of our congregation than "First." It went into the pile with eight other names.

We presented those names to a test group of congregation members representing as much diversity as we could gather. I encouraged

---

[5] Isaiah 62:4
[6] Mark 6:34

our group to not just think about what they liked, but to use five categories and rank the names according to how well they did in each category. The categories were: Reflects the heart of our church, Easy to understand for an outsider, Unique for our area, Starts a conversation, and Memorable. Each person ranked the potential names within these categories, and we came up with a "top three names" list. We then did the same thing with the church board, and they came up with their top three.

With this input, it came back to our Mission group. We made our own top three list. We were stuck, looking at all three lists, trying hard to make everyone happy. We all stood up, stretched, prayed, and looked at it one more time. Suddenly we looked at each other. We started to sing the line from the Christmas carol, "Do you see what I see?" Only one name was on all three lists. It was "Connection Christian Church." Clear as day. We were done and had our name to recommend to the board.

Joe and I began putting our presentation together for the board. That's when we discovered "Connection" was actually a very old name with deep roots in our church's denominational history. "The Christian Connexion" movement was created in 1810 when early American restorationist reformers, including James O'Kelly and Elias Smith, joined together. Their loose fellowship was called "The Christian Connexion." [7] The goal of the Connexion movement was two-fold: to advance reason as a means for interpreting the Bible, and to voluntarily connect churches for the sake of a unified witness to the gospel of Christ. That essence described our congregation. We wanted to draw and nurture people who were "thinking Christians" working out their own salvation as they connected individually to God. Yet we wanted people to be connected to deep fellowship in a Christian community that called them to be part of God's wider work in the world. "Connection" as a name not only catapulted us into the future but rooted us in our past.

The board accepted the new name unanimously. Then, as called for by our polity, the decision went before the congregation. They voted with ninety-one percent in favor of changing our name. Our Mission task force put together a video explaining the entirety of the process,

---

[7] You can read more about the Christian Connexion and their early journal here: https://www.ucc.org/ucc_roots_september_2019/

how the new name was rooted in our history, and how we might use the name for a logo and marketing. After watching that video, people said that it just made perfect sense. Our diehard, long-time pillars of the church said they were just relieved to see we weren't throwing out denominational identity, but rather updating it for reaching new generations.

I remember going over to Jackie Sue's house shortly after our new name was decided. She was one of those die hard, long-time church pillars. Remember the teeny-tiny woman on the search committee who prayed over our margaritas? She was struggling hard with all of this change. Jackie Sue was the granddaughter of founders of the church. Her family's history was tied up with the history of our church. All of this change was wearing on her.

I listened to her talk about her grief over leaving the building behind. She showed me pictures of her parents. Then, she told me that for the church to go on, she understood we had to move. Her blue eyes welling with tears, she gave me an envelope. Inside it was a pledge for the capital campaign to raise money for our renovation of the new building. I promised her we would make her parents, and her, proud of the legacy we carried into the future. I wish Jackie Sue had seen how it all turned out, but her emphysema worsened, and she died two weeks after we moved out of the downtown building. I think she would have loved what God has done with the new place.

We got to work on a logo and a simple motto that expressed the heart of our church. The motto came easily after three years of study and prayer about who we were called to be. "Connecting you to Christ and community" said it in a nutshell. The gospel story of feeding the multitudes that we had read throughout the process began to take shape anew in our midst. Disparate people, once on their own, being connected to Jesus and one another at a feast—that is the story we wanted to offer to our community.

A new logo was a bit trickier. Our denomination's logo, a red chalice with the cross of St. Andrew on it, was also our church's primary logo. But to the uninitiated, the Disciples of Christ logo looks like a wine glass with an "x" across it. Our new logo needed to give a nod to that chalice, and even more importantly, to the weekly open communion table it represented. But none of us knew how to express all of that in a contemporary way.

Again, we were stepping out in faith and our needs were met. Erin Patton, a professional graphic designer who grew up in our church, led our process. We wrangled with various designs, and settled on something both old and new: a chalice, though not one with an "x" on it, inside a circle. A cross is in the background becoming joined with the chalice, if you look closely. Once our team was happy with the logo, we showed it to people who don't attend our church to see what they saw in it. "Fresh," "open," and "welcoming" were the words that sold us on it. We decided to only use the old logo on our website in the "About Us" section, to indicate to denominational loyalists that we were indeed in the fold and not a start-up church with no ties to other churches. We chose signature colors so that we could develop a consistent branding of our church's representation in ads, social media, and signage. Our new logo, in a bright green and comfortable blue, became our signature stamp to represent our old-become-new identity.

When we relaunched the church into the community, we welcomed many guests and, eventually, new members to our congregation. They came because they liked the concept of Connection. They stayed because it was true. We were embodying the spirit we advertised. We truly cared for them and for this community. When your heart is expressed in your name, and your name is expressed in your heart, lives can be changed.

In Their Words by Penny Boss

The Boss family joined First Christian Church (Disciples of Christ) in 2004. We were the new kids on the block, as many FCC members were multigenerational. We were welcomed with open arms and quickly fell in love with the congregation, history, and traditions of our church. In a small congregation, it takes everyone to keep it running. I found many opportunities to be involved in the church and community outreach led by FCC. Starting out in smaller roles, I eventually served as a board moderator during a portion of the church transition—both in location and in name.

The congregation knew, when calling our new pastors, that relocation was in our future. Now leadership was suggesting a name change, and rebranding. No more "Disciples of Christ" in parenthesis or the red chalice? I'm sure many knew that a name change would be part of the process, but once again we were asking this congregation to make another change. And they did.

God was definitely at work in our church. It's easy to look back and see His handiwork and guidance throughout the process. The congregational survey, the hiring of a great interim pastor, the entire search process that led us to Joe and Dawn, their relocation to Odessa, the selling of a building, the purchasing of a new building, a new name and branding of a 112-year-old church, the time of meeting without a building—all of this taught us to lean on each other. We grew in our trust in God and in the assurance that we were not alone.

CHAPTER 7

Clink, Clink, Clink

You know how moving your own self is hard? Going through all of the stuff, getting it all packed up, making arrangements in a new space—it's a lot of work, not only physically but also emotionally. Imagine that with a 112-year-old congregation. And you know how it always feels bittersweet to leave a place you love and go to a new place you're going to love? Imagine seventy-five people of all ages going through the emotions of a move to a new house together.

Deciding what to take became the job of a special task force. We asked some of the longest-standing, most invested members of the church to help out. Pastor Joe spent hours with them, touring every closet, nook and cranny of our building, including the attic. They were prudent, though it was difficult. They truly wanted to take everything—every chandelier, every window with stained glass, every pretty thing decorating a table here and there. And proof that the Holy Spirit does still work in the church is that the task force agreed on three main things to carry to our new location.

First, the oldest stained glass in the building, which once hung in the original 1940s sanctuary, would find its third location in our new sanctuary. Its image of Jesus as a shepherd caring for the sheep, created just before World War II, was the grounding in our faith we needed. It reminded us that our Lord would lead us through green pastures, protect us in the presence of our enemies, and restore our souls.

The second major item we brought with us was all of our worship furniture. The 1960s-era carved maple would continue as our communion table and pulpit, connecting God's word and its servants from across the generations.

The third sentimental and symbolic thing we brought with us came by way of an accidental discovery. Once the movers came and everything was out of our buildings, Pastor Joe made one last sweep. He opened every closet door and poked his nose into every corner. When he opened a closet in the attic area above the sanctuary, he saw what looked like a few pieces of wood propped up in the corner. He moved closer and picked one up. It was then he discovered they were crosses. Three crosses to be exact, and they sure looked like the crosses that used to hang in the sanctuary when it was first erected in the 1960s. Joe remembered seeing them in past church pictorial directories. He wrapped them up in blankets and carried them out of the building to put in the back of our Mazda CX-9. Sure enough, they were the original big sanctuary's crosses, and we did not leave them behind. Those three crosses would hang in our new sanctuary's nave, across from the "Shepherd Jesus" stained glass. Two icons of our church's two most recent sanctuaries bookend the one we now occupy.

Though moving was hard and painful work, when our roots met our wings as a congregation, the Holy Spirit was palpable. Especially in people like Jeanne Ellen Keith. As a little girl, Jeanne Ellen rode the large bell up to the top of our downtown church's bell tower when it was erected in the 1940s. Now a beautiful woman in her eighties, Jeanne Ellen has a gentle voice enlivened by an unmistakable West Texas accent. Her blue eyes sparkle with a lifetime of proven faith. She kept reminding us that our current move would actually be to our church's fourth location over its more than a century of ministry. "You know," she'd say, "this will be our fourth location. God knows what He's doing." She was right. First, we met on the courthouse lawn. Next, we were in a tabernacle with a dirt floor, and finally, we were in the oldest of two buildings on our campus. Yes, the other three locations had been within a few blocks of each other, but still, she made her message heard. "The Lord will see us through just like He has many times before," she would say, and we believed her.

A saint in a church cannot be manufactured quickly. Jeanne Ellen has been growing in her faith and dedicating her life to our church's ministry for eighty years. A timely leader like that to spur the church on is a gift from God. She let us know: the church had changed before, and not only survived, but thrived. We could do this with God's help, she insisted. Thank heavens she did.

From Joe

When you die, you can't take your stuff with you. One difficult part of the journey was deciding what to do with our stuff—what and how much we should take with us. Some of us would've loved to bring all of our books, our stained-glass windows, our furniture. This is hard for a century-old congregation, with "In memory of…" inscribed not just on the windows, but on their hearts.

We went around the facilities, taking a picture of every feature, every artistic window, chandelier, and piece of art. We put them together in a photo album. We assembled a team of long-time folks to look through the pictures. It was amazing how some of them had not really noticed some artistic pieces. We started brainstorming how we could make our new building conform to our old things. But we re-evaluated. The goal became to only bring items that made sense in the new space, and that we could afford to move and use, and that would be honored in the new space. We did the same with our mundane items, furniture and kitchenware, etc. It was hard.

And we were not perfect. We got rid of so much in an estate sale, and yet we still brought too much with us. The most difficult items we left behind were features like stained-glass windows, given by families generations ago. But perspective helped. Though the church was a century old, folks mostly felt attached to items from ten to forty years ago because they were things from their own memories. In the end, we didn't take all our stuff with us, but if we had remained downtown and died our slow death, we wouldn't have taken all our stuff with us then either.

Our old downtown location had been a sacred space for many people. It was where parents had dedicated their babies, new Christians had experienced baptisms, weddings had been held, and loved ones had been mourned. Sacred places are a real thing. Celtic Christianity calls it a "thin place." This is where heaven and earth touch a little more closely than in your average grocery store. We followers of Jesus believe that his life began with the miracle of incarnation. We proclaim that God became a human being here on earth in Jesus. Incarnation means that humanity becomes a vessel for the Holy, and common places, like an animal's feeding trough, become revelatory locations. Really any place could be holy. But it sure helps to have some locations set aside as sacred. Our downtown location was a thin place for many. *It was not "just a building."*

Before everything was moved out, we held a great big last hurrah event in the old space. We invited all the old timers we could think of, including former pastors. We took a tour of every spot, from the sanctuary to the nursery, recalling memories, and thanking God for all that had been. Even, maybe especially, the kitchen held memories of spiritual family that could not be easily dismissed. As we walked prayerfully from room to room, we heard about long-dead saints of the church, guffawed at antics of youth group pranks, and shed tears in gratitude for all who had gone before. We gave thanks for being held by these walls, which whispered "God loves you" to so many people.

As any good Christians would, we held one last fellowship lunch. The potluck dishes were to die for, which was appropriate since we were, indeed, doing just that in a way. After filling our bellies and our spirits, we took a photo of everyone who attended.[8] We gathered on the front steps of the big sanctuary. Many long-time pillars of the church were there as well as newer faces of those who had bravely joined us for this journey. There were four young children in the picture, signs of God's trust in us to bring the gospel to new generations. The picture is priceless. Just four years later, many in the picture have passed on. Their courage to give Christian faith to the next generations speaks louder than ever from that photograph.

One estate sale and one garage sale later, the moving van came, and we packed it full of 112 years of ministry memories, equipment, and symbols. The beloved "Jesus as Shepherd" stained glass was professionally removed, and a regular window put back in its place. That did not go on the van but was carried separately. It was carefully placed in storage with our other treasures for our soon-to-be new church until it could all go where it was meant to be. The halls in the old downtown buildings began to feel empty and the reality that we would worship in much less reverent space was setting in. We used the church trailer to pack everything we needed for worship in the coming in-between season. The size of that small trailer compared to

---

[8] You can see that photo and get a feeling for what the move was like on our church's Youtube channel (Connection Christian Church Odessa).

the size of the moving van was telling. We were going to walk together without baggage for a while.

Our last worship service downtown was held on the last Sunday of the year, New Year's Eve. Everything was already moved out and the place echoed. We'd only kept out fifty folding chairs for worship and the sound equipment that would later go into the trailer. On this last day of 2017, we said goodbye to the old and hello to the new. We lit the Christ candle and remembered that the holy birth we just celebrated showed us that God will be with us in unexpected ways. We recalled the gospel story of Matthew chapter 2 where the wise men, having been warned in a dream not to return to Herod, went home by another way. We girded ourselves to do the same, to find a way other than the well-worn route we'd known for so long.

I thought I was prepared for my emotions, and the congregation's too. We sang the familiar Christmastide hymns with gusto, our voices resonating in our near-empty space. This was almost fun! But then the offering came. We passed the two brass plates we'd held out for this occasion while our pianist played a jazzy version of "Go, Tell It on the Mountain" on the portable, electric keyboard. "Down in a lowly manger, the humble Christ was born," I was singing. And then I heard a strange sound. It was a clinking sound, but heavier than someone putting change in the metal plate. I heard it again, more of a clunk than a clink. And again! Clink, clunk, clink! When the deacon brought the plates forward, I looked in to see what the unusual offerings were.

It was then unbidden tears came. For it was keys, keys in the offering plate! The beloved, tireless leaders of our church were turning in their keys to the downtown buildings. They were doing one last, hard thing. They were letting their keys go and entrusting them as an offering to God, along with all their years of service in this location. I fished my keys out of my purse and added them to the pile.

In Their Words by Jeanne Ellen Keith

I remember when the original sanctuary of First Christian Church was built. It was in the Spring of 1942, and my family lived between the First Methodist Church and First Baptist Church and next to where the First Christian Church was built. I remember my mother cooked a hot meal daily for the construction crew and was always there to handle any emergency. I remember riding the bells up in the tower when they were being installed. My brother and I were both raised and baptized in the church, as well as my four children. I remember many celebrations, luncheons, and Spaghetti Day fundraisers. I also remember many funerals that were given at the church, including for both of my parents and my husband. My daughter was married in the church.

When we began discussing different options of either staying where we were or relocating and branching off, yes, it was difficult. It was hard to think about leaving this building that I had witnessed being built. Not only was I raised there but I raised my own children there. Yet I felt like God was moving our congregation out of our comfort zone for a reason. He was trying to tell us it was time to move on. Our pastors were a big help in encouraging us all to understand God's call. Even though I was apprehensive at first, I felt like we needed to put our trust in God because He had a plan. I will always carry the memories with me of First Christian Church. Now, I will make new memories. God told us not to put our trust in material things, but to trust in him always. Something else I truly believe is that God is not a specific building, but wherever there are two or more gathered in fellowship, God will be there also.

CHAPTER 8

The Cafetorium Wilderness

For the three years before our relocation began, our congregation practiced doing church in weird places. First, we met weekly for Bible study at a little wine room in town. They set out chairs for us in a corner with a sign that said "Church" propped on the table. Not only was the conversation and study enjoyable, but we often had interesting conversations with the patrons. They were intrigued and listening in on our discussions. Sometimes we prayed with someone in need of support, like the mother whose son had just headed off to Army boot camp. She saw us taking a moment to bow our heads in prayer and rushed over to add his name to our hearts.

We also met for weekly Bible studies at the Chick-fil-A, at a local coffee shop, and even at the grocery store, by the deli bar. Plus, for over a year, we held Dinner Church once a month at a local Italian place. This Sunday evening gathering had a new visitor or three nearly every time we came together. People were just curious about church at a restaurant. And we began the tradition of "Ashes to Go" on Ash Wednesday. We surprised and blessed people with the sign of the cross and a prayer in gas stations and on street corners. We even started "Coffee on the Corner" at the traffic intersection by our new location during the cooler months, sharing coffee, water, and prayer with morning commuters. We offered church in odd places to get us out of our box, and also to get connected to our community. We learned that *church is not just in a building*. We practiced that truth until we knew it deep in our bones. Church can be anywhere two or three are gathered in Jesus' name.

Thinking about gathering in weird places became a part of our church's culture. Yet being out of the box all the time was a daunting prospect. We prayed hard over where we would meet for worship and Sunday school classes temporarily while our new building was being renovated. Our minds were open to just about anywhere. Practically speaking though, we couldn't get too crazy. We needed a place where we could set up and take down our equipment easily and quickly. We also required a place that was wheelchair accessible, with good restrooms, and a way to use a sound system and a screen. Perhaps most importantly, our temporary digs must not break the bank. We considered a movie theatre in town, for example, which would have been fun except that it cost $2000 to rent each Sunday. Our best option became the elementary school four blocks down from our new location. It had a cafetorium with metal folding chairs we could borrow. It had a sound system and a screen. And the price was reasonable. Plus, we might get to develop a relationship with some of the teachers and staff. So, we moved into the Blanton Elementary School cafetorium.

If you haven't had the pleasure, a cafetorium is a school cafeteria with a stage in it. We rented it for three hours every Sunday, which was far less work in property maintenance than keeping an aging, 30,000-square-foot church building and campus operational seven days a week. We were traveling light. That was the upside. On the downside, the chairs were the worst. Our butts quickly grew tired of hard, cold, metal folding chairs with no cushion. If we'd known how long we were going to be there, we would have invested in some church-logo cushions, the kind you take to stadiums. Also, the aesthetics were less than ideal, and the acoustics were super live. But you could see the schoolteachers who came in on weekends to work and marvel at their dedication. That was pure inspiration.

Our congregation began the new year of 2018 in that cafetorium. As we set up for our first Sunday, I could feel the butterflies rising in my stomach. Would people find us? Would everyone make the shift? That was probably too much to hope for, but I hoped, nonetheless. Indeed, when all was said and done, only two regular worshippers decided not to come along. (Six months later, one returned, confessing that she had "been in a tizzy" but had gotten over it). That first Sunday at the elementary school, sixty folks showed up for worship. It was a powerful, palpable manifestation of faithfulness. Yes, church buildings were meaningful, but church people—that's who we couldn't live without.

There were David and Bill and Dan, deacons in title and heart, setting up folding chairs. Gina, youth Sunday school teacher, was bringing donuts down the hallway to the corner where her class would now meet. Sarah was setting up for children's Sunday school in the school library. And Larry had figured out how to get our old coffee maker brewing on a card table he'd set up right by the front door. The faces of our friends shone out from an elementary school the same as from an eighty-year-old church building. We already knew this truth—that people are what matters—from our experiences at the wine bar, the coffee shop, the Italian restaurant, Ashes to Go, and other places. Now it was being confirmed at the cafetorium. "For where two or three connect with one another in my name, I am there in their midst," Jesus says in Matthew 18:20. Jesus was with us.

We embraced the theme of "wilderness" for our time at Blanton Elementary. Like the Hebrew people traversing a desert for forty years, moving from slavery to freedom, we were moving from a known to an unknown, trusting life would be more free. Like Jesus taking forty days to pray before beginning his public ministry, we were leaning into God in new ways to gain strength for our impact for the gospel in our community. It was an in-between time. The old wineskins were gone, and the new ones weren't on yet. We were a turtle without a shell, a church without a building.

In her perfectly titled book, *How to Lead When You Don't Know Where You're Going*, Susan Beaumont writes that liminal times are "dangerous, alluring, and sacred."[9] Beaumont says transition times are *dangerous* because it is uncomfortable to operate without set expectations and limitations. We are especially vulnerable to quick fixes and ill-intentioned agendas to get us out of the discomfort. I was afraid people would leave to go to a more conventional church due to the discomfort of the cafetorium. But no one did.

Beaumont says liminality is *alluring* because it is exciting to throw off what was and have a blank slate. Remember the Calvin and Hobbes cartoon? The last scene ever created draws the beloved series to a close. It shows Calvin the boy and Hobbes the tiger on a sled at the top of a freshly-snowed scene. Calvin says to Hobbes, "It's a magical

---

[9] Susan Beaumont, *How to Lead When You Don't Know Where You're Going,* Rowman & Littlefield, 2019

world, old buddy. Let's go exploring!"[10] When everything is fresh and new, unmarked by mistake or achievement, it can be a heady time.

We found Beaumont's words of "dangerous" and "alluring" to be true, but especially we found her third word to be spot on: "sacred." Somehow the elementary school cafetorium became a cocoon for God to do what God does. Wilderness is a place with no baggage and much to learn. Our own cafetorium wilderness offered God room and time to recreate us anew. Without the structure of a building, our congregation was moldable clay in the hands of the very trustworthy, sculpting Holy Spirit.

Who were we now, without all of our stuff? This was the question of the wilderness. The freedom was difficult, and wonderfully necessary. Where would we keep our nursery? In the kindergarten hallway of course. Was it ideal? No. Was it a better location than across the alley? Yes! What would we do about Sunday school classes? The school's library became five Sunday school classes for all ages, giving plenty of grace for other groups' laughter for which your group didn't hear the joke. What about where to have our Ash Wednesday and Holy Week services, since our arrangement with the school was Sundays only? Ecumenical partnerships came to the rescue as we shared worship with our local Presbyterian friends. How would we do our annual Christmas Smorgasbord party? We'd move it to Sunday mornings and eat like kings at 10am. It was a cafetorium, after all!

We even let go of the concept of a church office for a time as our staff worked from home. We found we didn't need a landline phone. We transferred that number to a mobile device, and never looked back. Not everything that needed to be adapted was that easy-breezy, of course. It was a special joy to have the youth group meet at the pastors' home, yet that did require more regular housekeeping than we normally would do. Plus, the neighbors started to wonder if we just kept having children or were running a foster home!

The most painful thing about being in temporary space was the death of two congregation members during that wilderness season. We had to hold their memorial services at funeral homes because we did not yet have a building ready to host grieving families. It was disappointing

---

[10] Bill Watterson, *It's a Magical World: A Collection of Calvin and Hobbes*, Andrews & McNeel, 1996

to not be able to honor those beloved saints with a proper church funeral. The wilderness hurts sometimes.

The sheer logistics of worshipping in an elementary school were also challenging. Everything our church needed to lead worship was packed up in a small trailer. Having to set up and take down our "church in a box" which was really "church out of the box" was labor intensive. We set up and took down chairs, the communion table, a screen, a sound system, a coffee bar, our signage, our musical instruments, and all kinds of other things every Sunday. Our dedicated helpers grew weary. But no matter if they were enduring a dust storm, freezing cold, or sweltering temperatures, our deacons put up and took down signs on the school's outdoor chain link fences every Sunday. They announced "Connection Christian Church Worships Here, Sundays 11am." And our new location was so visible that people actually noticed that sign *and came to check us out.*

The new people who came during our wilderness wanderings tripled the few guests we had received every now and then downtown. So many folks wanted to see what was going on. We discovered that people are drawn to an opportunity to get in on the ground floor of something beginning, rather than trying to catch a moving train. People even became members of our church during this time. Some of our current strong leaders in the church came from our days in the cafetorium wilderness. We built up momentum for our launch in surprising ways. We grew not only in attendance but also in spirit. Most of our congregation, myself included, just couldn't believe that God would send us so many new people when we were worshipping without so much as a proper altar, much less a decent piano.

When God created the world in Genesis chapter 1, the scripture says, "God sensed that it was good."[11] I began to notice that church was good, just as we were, without much else. Caring for each other and those whom God brought as sweet surprises was good. Even sitting on cold, metal folding chairs while we spent time in the wilderness had its good points. At least no one fell asleep during worship! Folding those chairs up after worship so we could go and live out our faith was good.

Remember the tabernacle described in Exodus chapter 25? It was a temporary place of worship, to be set up as God's people were

---

[11] Genesis 1:31.

moving forward in obedience to God's call. Having our identity not in a building but in how we were responding to God's call sharpened our faith profoundly. Who were we, without our buildings? Without even a chair to sit in? We were people trying to follow Jesus and inviting others to discover him too. That's it, and that's more than enough. The spirit of tabernacling changed our spiritual DNA.

There were many blessings in that "wandering in the wilderness" time. But it went on and on. Our estimate of "six months tops" turned into fourteen months. We pushed and pushed our contractor to hurry. This was a remodel and not new construction, which meant there were issues we could not have anticipated. A low point for me was when we realized we would need to do Christmas Eve service with our Presbyterian friends. I had promised the congregation that surely, we would be in by Christmas. I had to eat my words, and they were not a tasty Advent snack. But the gracious Westminster Presbyterian Church took us in for Christmas Eve worship, like Mary and Joseph with no place to lay their heads. And soon enough, our baby was born.

In Their Words by Marlon Fick

When I arrived in Texas to begin working at the university, I left behind a trail that crossed cities and continents. My life had always been about places, not people—and from quite an early age. I attended high school in Paris, France. I served in the Peace Corps in the Congo of Africa. I lived in Mexico City for fifteen years. A year in Pakistan. Two years in China. Three years among the Navajos. I was attracted to places and often overlooked my neighbors entirely. I am ashamed to confess this.

During my first week in Odessa, Texas, which isn't quite as exotic as Shanghai or Paris, I asked a colleague where I might find a church that would have someone like me for a member. "Connection Christian Church," he said. I didn't know it then, but that moment would change my life forever, and for the better. In the bitter winter of 2018, we met on cold metal chairs in an elementary school. It was awful. Why had this congregation abandoned a beautiful church downtown? What was up with that? And why would they be in the process of converting a commercial property? Strange. But for some reason—a mystery to me then—I kept coming, every Sunday without fail. I missed the grand organ music I'd grown up with, the comfortable pews, the hymnals that taught me how to read notes, the gorgeous stained glass. I felt as if I had gone from Notre Dame Cathedral, where I had attended services as a teenager, to the gutter.

Slowly, gradually, it became obvious how God was working in my life through Connection Christian Church. God was manifesting his love through people, not places. I would not trade Odessa for anywhere, not because there is any "thing" in particular here, but because there is a family who worships together and practices the art of loving. This love gave my life something I lost a long time ago—a sense of belonging.

CHAPTER 9

The Key Ingredient

In chapter 15 of John's gospel, Jesus said, "By this, everyone will know you are my followers: if you have love among one another." But loving each other is not the only thing a church should do. Jesus also said, "Care for my sheep;" and "To the extent that you did these for one of the least among my brothers and sisters, you did it for me;" and "Go, teaching every group of people, and washing them in the name of the Father, Son, and Sacred Wind," to name a few.[12]

Our vision is directed outward by Jesus' commands. A church that only focuses on loving those who attend will shrivel up and die from twisting in on itself. The joke among clergy is that if your church prides itself on being friendly above all else, it's a sure sign that your church will not be around much longer. Mutual love is not the only thing needed for a church to be truly and fully alive. But a church that just focuses on doing all the other good things Jesus said has no internal combustion to move the church forward unless love for one other is happening. Through Connection's sacred days of transition, we anchored ourselves by loving each other and whoever came into our midst.

Our church loves hard. What this looks like depends on the need. Our elders have "shepherding groups" they call on to make sure everyone hears from the church and receives prayer for their needs on the regular. Every adult is invited to participate in one of six adult Bible study groups that provide additional community. Our children and youth are connected into ministry groups for their age, and we are engaged with them twice weekly. Ministry teams serve as deacons, food bank volunteers, and choir members, as well as in other forms of ministry. We seek to overcommunicate by sending out weekly

---

[12] John 21:17, Matthew 25:40, Matthew 28:19.

emails, texts, and social media posts. We even still snail-mail a monthly newsletter. These are the structural ways we connect. But something less structural and more organic happens as well. When the church has lovingly cared for a person, that person often becomes a part of doing the caring.

Our church, as a part of the Disciples of Christ denomination, takes communion every Sunday, as God intended it. (*Smile.*) Maybe you have taken communion using the chiclets method—the small, hard, oyster crackers that are convenient and tasteless. It works fine, but it does not leave you wanting more. Well, decades ago, Lynne Norwood, one of our deacons, decided enough was enough. She was done with eating Styrofoam in the name of Jesus! Lynne was a dedicated elementary school educator who knew how to improvise. She experimented with some ideas and came up with using pie crust—yes, pie crust—for communion crackers! Now we have deacons who are trained by other deacons on how to make and roll out the pie crust, score it, bake it, store it, and bring it to the church to put in our communion trays. And let me tell you: once you have eaten pie crust communion, you definitely want more.

In the same way we raised our standards for communion, we also raised them when it comes to what it means to be loved by a church. We hope to love in a way that makes people want to receive and give more love. When someone comes to worship or Bible study or to volunteer for the first time, we make every effort to get their name and remember it. We ask for a way to stay in touch. And, we have a little welcome gift we give them on the spot or drop off at their house, whichever works. When someone joins, we celebrate with a lot of hoorays and applause. When someone gets baptized, there's always a cake. When someone is sick, a meal is on their porch. When someone is unable to join us for worship in person anymore due to age or illness, we bring communion to them. When a baby is on the way, a shower is most definitely in order. When a death occurs, we send cards, not just right then, but throughout the next year. When a job is lost, networks go into action finding another place of employment. When mental illness throbs, listening ears and hugs are all around. We love each other well.

But caring for each other isn't all rainbows and butterflies. Sometimes the emotions ran high as we made these major steps toward transformation. People who love each other got mad at each other. Occasionally someone threatened to leave; sometimes, folks' feelings got hurt. Giving each other the space to lament, to be frustrated or angry or sad, is a part of loving one another. The discomfort of wrangling with change took grit and grace from the whole congregation. Occasionally, loving well means confrontation in the kindest, but firmest, way possible.

One of the saints of our church is Ronald Bennett, a beloved piano teacher and arts advocate in our community. Ronald's quick wit and impeccable manners delighted our most elderly Sunday school class, where he taught for years. This feisty group was comprised of people in their eighties and nineties, for whom change can be a lot to ask. Every week on Thursdays, he faithfully called every member of his class to check on them, and to keep them apprised on was happening at the church. When they answered the phone, Ronald did not ever say it was him. Instead, he said, "Tell me five good things." Then he waited for them to come up with a list of gratitude. He always threw in a groaner joke or two before the call ended.

Ronald has dementia now. But before his memory started to fade, thankfully, he remembered clearly when our church had been vibrant, and he knew the difference between the heyday of our church and the struggle we were facing before our relocation. Ronald was a cheerleader for our transformation process. He imagined what was possible for our congregation's future and he trusted the church leadership to be faithful in realizing those possibilities. He sent his pastors regular cards of encouragement and hope. He prayed fervently for the change. But perhaps the best thing he did was take people to lunch.

When someone would get in a snit or stop coming to church for a while, Ronald noticed. He would call them up and say, "Let's go to lunch." I don't know how many times Ronald did this. It was an automatic response for him. He met the offended party at Delicias Mexican Restaurant. Over hot, fresh tortillas, he listened carefully to hurt feelings, grievances, or whatever his beloved friend needed to say. Then, he patiently, lovingly, explained why the best way for our church to be faithful was to make this move. By the time he picked up the bill, a friendship was still intact, and the church had gained a new advocate for hope. His "let's go to lunch" strategy never failed. I sometimes wonder if going to lunch together might solve more problems than we think.

Now, our elders go visit Ronald in his assisted living center to bring him communion from our church. Some of them never worshiped in the downtown church and didn't know Ronald in his most vibrant days. But because Ronald advocated for our church's future when we needed it most, our church is able to deploy Christian leaders to care for him today.

Ronald had his finger on the pulse of the older generations in our church. When I get the privilege of checking the mail, I look for their familiar handwriting. At least monthly, there will be a check in the mail from one of our elderly folks. Often there's a note, "Praying for you!" or "Sending love!" Seeing their handwriting always feels like a hug from above. They love their Jesus and his church so much that love pours right out from the mailbox.

To paraphrase the biblical book of James, our church loves not just with words but in actions. Each year I review our financial donations so Joe and I can write thank you notes for those going the extra mile to give. Inevitably, there is someone who just joined, or had a rough year, yet there they are, giving unexpectedly. Sadly, sometimes when people work on a church staff, they can get jaded about church folk. But for me at Connection, seeing what happens behind the scenes keeps my hope in God's work through the church high. Because every now and then I get to see *how our people love when no one else but God is looking*. This congregation not only loves each other in obvious ways; we also quietly and sacrificially give money to support our church and its ministries.

Our church was drawing money from our endowment to meet expenses for two decades. Once we relocated, we became able to more than meet our expenses, increase our outreach giving, and encourage our staff with raises, partly because we reduced our expenses in a more modern building, but mostly because our congregation has grown, not only in number, but in love. You know how everyone loves to hate 2020, the year of the COVID-19 pandemic? That was our church's largest year of giving *in history*. That year, our congregation gave of themselves to Christ and his church in practical, generous ways. They loved with all they had, including their wallets.

Joe and I are tithers, so we are used to being among the top givers in congregations where we have served. But in this congregation, we have stiff competition. A mark of the congregation's maturity as Christians is that they get that following Jesus means putting your money where your mouth is. When new people join in, of course we do not tell them they need to dig deep. Yet that vibe is in the air and folks feel the congregation's commitment. Love is contagious in a good way.

Two years ago, a new couple came to worship with us after swearing off church decades ago. They once counted themselves as atheists. But the kindness they experienced from people in our church started working on them and in them. As they began to trust they were loved as they are, they began to give. Then they decided to tithe, giving ten percent of their income. No one ever pressured them about this. They heard about giving and they saw giving all around them. Maybe most importantly, they experienced abundant love from God through our church.

They shared their testimony with the congregation recently. "We don't need so much stuff anymore. God just fills those empty spaces so much better than things!" they proclaimed, and the place broke out in applause.

Remember when we bought our new-to-us building and sold our previous buildings for nearly the same amount? That even trade was not the end of the expenses of our relocation. By the time we raised the roof for a sanctuary, fire sprinkled the whole thing, and added two large bathrooms, the price kept adding up. Remodeling the new location cost an additional $1.5 million beyond the purchase of the building. We did a capital campaign to cover some of those costs, setting a goal of $300,000. Over $500,000 was given. We now have a loan from our denomination's lending ministry, Church Extension. A debt reduction campaign three years later helped us whittle our loan down another $300,000 to an amount the congregation can easily manage in the coming years. We are in good financial shape, thanks be to God.

That's because love makes the difference: loving God, loving each other, and loving the future generations of our church. The love is easy to see.

In Their Words **by Gina Yarbrough**

From the beginning of our time at this church, forty-two years ago, we have felt the love of Jesus and his followers here. One of our neighbors invited our family and another young family to visit the church, and we all felt right at home in the Christian Church (Disciples of Christ). We have never looked back.

Over the years I believe that either I and/or my husband have served on just about every church committee or group. We have served God and our neighbors, not just because Christ commanded it, but because he modeled it, and it feels so right. For the past seven years I served as our Membership Chair, which covers many aspects of people's lives, from the time they join the church to their deaths. As congregants experience the ups and downs of life, our ministry team tries to be there for them and their families. It has been a joy to serve my neighbors.

My husband and I have witnessed many changes in the church over the years—in attendance numbers, pastors, ministry styles, outreach projects, facility upgrades, and finally in location. Although some members were quite distressed about the thought of moving, I personally did not feel much anxiety. It was time for change. Church growth specialists told us many years ago that we needed to move closer to people in our community who would be more receptive to our message.

Our pastors and transition teams took us slowly and thoughtfully through the lengthy relocation process. Although Pastors Dawn and Joe must have had many sleepless nights, their consistent attitudes of optimism, caring, and enthusiasm have carried us through the many inevitable challenges. Thanks be to God for providing leadership and resources to help us successfully transition into a bigger, more inclusive, more loving congregation. Thanks be to God for so many new lives that have been touched by God's love in this new, welcoming place!

CHAPTER 10

Y'all Means All

While we were going through the process of deciding to move, there was an elephant in the room. Joe and I brought up the subject of Queer people in the church back when we were interviewing with the search committee. At that time, former Texas governor Rick Perry had recently said he believed people "have the ability to decide not to be gay."[13] One of the church's leaders joked and asked if we thought you could "pray the gay away." Joe and I said, all joking aside, that we did not believe that. We answered that we practiced an inclusive approach to ministry with Queer people and would do so in Odessa if called. The people in the room were at peace with that.

What we discovered after some time in the congregation was that this church, like many other churches, practiced church with the "don't ask, don't tell" policy. A beloved elderly man in the church was "very probably" gay; no one had ever asked him. A benefactor of the church had a lesbian daughter; a beloved Sunday school teacher had a gay son. But the conversation about the intentional inclusion of LGBTQ+ people had not formally come up in the congregation.

Joe and I had been pastoring in Odessa for less than a year when the Supreme Court ruled in June of 2015 that same-sex marriage would be legal in the United States. Our tenure was too short for us to assume how the congregation felt about gay marriage. *All we knew for sure was that it is very difficult to lead a church with your head in the sand.* So, we asked our elders, "What do you want your pastors to do if a same-sex couple asks that we marry them?"

---

[13] Sean Sullivan, "Rick Perry Doesn't Back Down from Comparing Homosexuality to Alcoholism", washingtonpost.com, June 16, 2014, https://www.washingtonpost.com/news/post-politics/wp/2014/06/16/rick-perry-doesnt-back-down-from-comparing-homosexuality-to-alcoholism/

Meanwhile, someone new began attending our church. Mark Tenniswood started showing up because we offered our unused sanctuary space to nonprofit organizations if they needed larger venues. Mark's small community theatre company, Mark10, took us up on it. Their first performance was *Coraline*, a spooky children's play. The event was attended by hundreds of Ector County ISD students who were each given a copy of the book. It even corresponded with a visit from author Neil Gaiman himself. Yes, we live in a sometimes magical and surprising town!

Mark10's second project was *The Laramie Project*, which chronicles a hate crime against a young gay man. The local TV news stations reported that this controversial-for-our-area play was being performed at our church. I spent some extra time in prayer over that, yet no one in the congregation said a word about it.

Mark became a dear friend to our congregation. He started coming to worship regularly, bringing his infectious smile and caring heart. We borrowed his theatrical prowess for the children's Christmas pageant, of course. Mark was the first openly gay person who became a regular, integral part of our congregation. He was married to a wonderful man named Shannon. I thank God for Mark for many reasons. I am grateful most especially because when the elders started studying what our church's response to same-sex marriage would be, it wasn't a hypothetical about people we didn't know. It was about Mark. Mark, who had a lovely tenor voice, was kind to a fault, and always brought his sweet dog Sasha Underfoot to church fellowship picnics.

As we were getting to know Mark, our elders were studying the Bible and praying about the inclusion of LGBTQ+ people in our church. In the Disciples of Christ denomination, elders and pastors are partners. Elders are, in a sense, volunteer pastors. Their number one job is to tend to the spiritual health of a congregation. That's why Joe and I asked the elders, "What do you want us to say if we are asked by a same-sex couple to marry them?" For nearly a year, we studied the six passages that seem to reference homosexuality in scripture and their current and historical interpretations. We also listened to each other's stories of friends and family we loved who were gay.

Near the end of our discernment, almost all of the elders were ready to become a more intentionally inclusive church. They suggested that we share the same study we had done as elders with the congregation in a summarized fashion. So, over a month's time, we held congregational conversations discussing what the Bible says about LGBTQ+ people and the church. We asked the congregation to let our elders know privately as well as in a group setting what their wisdom was about this. Then, having heard feedback from the congregation, the elders decided. It sounds monumental, but really their decision was simple: Over the past one hundred ten years, we'd never explicitly excluded Queer folks, our elders had never told our pastors whom to marry, and we were not going to start. Joe and I breathed a prayer of gratitude for these practical leaders. Yet still we weren't sure how welcomed *and* affirmed Queer folks would be.

Then the call came early one morning that Mark and his dog had died in a car accident. We held Mark's funeral in the big sanctuary. It was the fullest I had ever seen it. Our church choir sang "Seasons of Love" from *Rent*. Mark's husband Shannon and Mark's mother Kathleen carried his ashes down the aisle together. They then set the urn on our communion table. Shannon spoke with amazing passion and poise as he gave homage to "the only man I've ever loved." I looked out upon the sanctuary and saw gay couples, out and closeted, mourning a local hero to them. And I looked out into the faces of our congregation and saw our hearts burst wide open.

Not every single one of course. In the Disciples of Christ denomination, we pride ourselves on holding diverse opinions in love. At no moment then or now did we say, "You need to believe this or you're not a good fit here anymore." And yet, it was important to Joe and me as pastors that before the church's relocation, we were clear. We did not want to go through all the soul-wrenching work of rebirthing this congregation just to have a split over gay marriage once we got to a new chapter. So as the congregation decided to move, our Mission team intentionally developed our wording about who we are. We wanted to be forthright in our marketing. Here's what we said (it's on our website if you want to look).[14]

> "We celebrate who you are: male and female, single and married, gay and straight, brown, black, and white, Democrat and

---

[14] www.odessaconnection.church

Republican, churchy and not churchy, Red Raider, Longhorn, and Horned Frog—welcome!

To be crystal clear: We believe John 3:17, which says God didn't send Jesus to judge the world, but to save it. Ain't nobody got time to judge when we're just trying to love. Men and women serve equally in all capacities in our church. LGBT people too. Hablar español or ingles. Whatever your family looks like—yes! If you aren't sure you believe yet—yes! Come on and test our welcome."

Now when people join our church, Joe or I have this conversation with them: "You need to know that this is a church where LGBTQ+ people are fully welcomed and affirmed. I don't want you to get involved and then be shocked by that. Now, you do not have to agree with same-sex marriage. We have room for you. Yet we ask you to give dignity and grace to others. It's essential." And I have the same conversation with openly LGBTQ+ folk: "Before you join, let me tell you that our leadership, including your pastors, are welcoming and affirming of all sexual and gender orientations. Not every single person who comes here is, nor do we ask them to be. We think this is the best place for them to be loved and to grow also. But if anyone ever makes you feel unloved here...please, we want to know. Making this a safe space for you is important to us."

About a year after we moved into our new building, we published our in-house church photo directory, the first one in ten years. You could see the change. It's obvious to everyone; the witness flies off the page. More than ten percent of our households are openly LGBTQ+ households. We look like our community, at least in that way. Praise God from whom all blessings flow!

Our church had done the work to be ready to be truly open and we were chomping at the bit to get into our building so we could open it to all people. We had hoped and prayed to be in our new building within a year, but that year had come and gone. Our grand opening was reset for Palm Sunday of 2019. Jesus' "grand opening" on the scene in Jerusalem would be our grand opening day as well. As we began planning for that in earnest in January, our family life shifted significantly.

Joe's mother was entering the late stages of Alzheimer's disease. With Joe's dad, we moved her from her home in the Houston area, into a care facility near us. It was an excruciatingly painful time as we said goodbye to his mom as we knew her, yet physically she was still with us. The care facility in our town was unequipped for her and three months later, she returned home to a more suitable setting.

Meanwhile, the church's launch was happening. It was strange to be at such a zenith in our ministry while at such a tough season in our home life. Sometimes pastors have to just be people. Okay, all the time, but it's messier at some junctures than at others.

The congregation's enthusiasm carried us forward during that time. As we approached Holy Week of 2019, there were commercials to make, social media campaigns to launch, furniture pieces to arrange, and last-minute pictures to place. Our elders and I prayer-walked the new neighborhood. We sent postcards to invite our neighbors to come to worship on Palm Sunday. We sent out invitations to the big day to everyone in the church and multiple community leaders.

We did a soft opening worship service a few weeks before launch day. We nearly filled our sanctuary with just our congregation. Deciding how big to make the sanctuary had been partly a matter of how much space we had available to use within the confines of our remodeled building. But it was also a decision about right-sizing.

Our previous sanctuary seating of 400 was obviously too much. We were averaging about 65 people in attendance at our worship at the elementary school. We planned for a space that could seat 170 max. It would seem full at 80% capacity, so that meant we could seat about 135 people comfortably. Once we neared that, we planned to start another worship service.

When our soft opening attendance was at 80, we took another leap and moved to two service offerings before the grand opening for the community. We wanted more room for people to join us.

If there was a time to make a change to our worship schedule, the time was before we opened to the community. Our previous schedule when we were downtown had included two services, not because of a need for room, but because of two different style preferences in the church. Our 9 a.m. contemporary service was attended by around 15 folks and our 11 a.m. traditional service drew about 40. Some people went to both services. In our new location, we switched those two services, moving to 9 a.m. for our classic service with hymns and 11 a.m. for our contemporary service with our band. Between the services are our Bible study classes for children, youth, and adults. Children's worship, based on the program *Godly Play*, is offered during both worship times.[15] Once that schedule was decided, we began two services on Easter Sunday, immediately following our launch service on Palm Sunday.

Then, we made a TV commercial. In our area of 250,000 people, with three local TV stations, commercials are not cost-prohibitive. We often get on the news for free by issuing press releases whenever we are doing something to connect with our community, like offering a vaccination clinic or collecting items for refugee families. While free is good, sometimes a little output of cash is called for, like when launching a new location for your church. With some volunteered expertise in our congregation, and using our own talent as actors, we took on the adventure of making an ad for the gospel we want to share. Our vision came from a commercial made for Canada's 150th birthday. In that commercial, a child and her mother are returning home to their apartment. No one speaks to them in the elevator, and they walk, alone, to their apartment and shut the door. But a second later, they come out of their apartment with a table which they set down in the hallway. Then they start knocking on their neighbors' doors. Before you know it, others bring out chairs and food, and where there was no connection, now there is a diverse family having dinner in the hallway.[16]

Our church's commercial showed familiar places in our community: a well-used park playground, a beloved pond, a popular grocery store, and a replica of Stonehenge at our town's university. In all these places, we showed members of our congregation reaching out to give invitation cards to people jogging or playing or sitting around. The last scene was a very long table on our parking lot in front of our new church building. People who had been invited were gathering around,

---

[15] https://www.godlyplayfoundation.org

[16] You can see Canada's commercial here: https://www.youtube.com/watch?v=yLsSy64xILI

welcoming each other. Then we grabbed hands and said grace as the commercial ended with a voiceover, "Life is meant to be shared. At Connection Christian Church, we connect you to Christ and community. Come and see this Sunday at 9 and 11 a.m. There's a place at the Table for you." It really captured what we are about in 30 seconds.[17]

The guests who came after that TV spot aired overwhelmed us. We were not prepared for how many people would try out a church just because they saw it on TV. Many also watched the roof on our new building go up and came because they were curious. People kept coming in to worship and saying, "This used to be my (or my dad's or my kid's) doctor's office!" We did not realize how many people were disconnected and looking for a church home. We welcomed 10 to 15 guests every Sunday in our first six months.

We also were not ready for how many children we would meet. In our downtown location, we no longer had a traditional Vacation Bible School because there were only four children regularly attending our church. Instead, we offered VBS at the Boys and Girls Club in our community. There we could employ our "stations" of crafts, games, Bible story, snacks, and music, while giving their staff a two-hour morning break. This was an effective way to bless our community and to keep our children's ministry muscles strong while we had so few children.

We flexed those fit muscles in our new location. That summer, we held our first full-fledged Vacation Bible School at our church to see how it would go. We advertised registration on social media and served 94 children that week. At last, we were fully open, in every way, to everybody.

In Their Words by Rosyln Ross

When Tracy and I wanted to join Connection Christian Church, we were admittedly a bit nervous. After all, would this church actually welcome us openly, as we are, a same-sex couple? What a concept! Our prior experience with Connection was knowing

---

[17] You can see our commercial here: https://www.youtube.com/watch?v=gQL-CdR_e0Kk

Mark Tenniswood, one of the first theatre folks we met when we moved here, and watching *The Laramie Project* at the church downtown. Then we met the Weaks family through the Permian Playhouse. Little did we know how impactful that would be in our lives.

We had not been visiting the church for very long before we realized everyone did welcome us, individually and as a couple. Not one snub or nasty look or anything that made us feel unwelcome. Quite the opposite, as a matter of fact. We both felt as if everyone truly cared about us and everyone else around us.

In May 2021, my wife and I were asked if we would be interested in representing our church at Odessa's Pride Festival. What an honor that was, and we jumped at the chance. It was in August, hot as hot gets in West Texas, which made for a long day. We would both do it again in a heartbeat. We were so proud to represent Connection Christian Church. Our foray into the world of Pride festivals was very well received. Every person who came to our booth was interested in hearing about the church, and wanted to know: were we as a church truly accepting of everyone? We spent the entire day telling people that God loves them as they are, and so will everyone at Connection. We hugged, prayed, and cried with a whole lot of people who were looking for validation, recognition, and a friendly face. We were well received, and one of the busiest booths there. It was satisfying in a way that really can't be described. It was soul-deep and so fulfilling to be able to spread the word that God and we love people, just where they are and who they are. There is no way to describe the feeling of acceptance and love we experienced and continue to experience through connecting with God and community, not in spite of who we are, but *because* of who we are.

CHAPTER 11
Where Does It Hurt?

Our church's big launch day came on Palm Sunday of 2019. I got there early to make sure everything was ready to go and found that three other church members had beaten me to it. David, Bill, and Dan, the team who oversaw the set-up of our cafetorium worship at the elementary school, were there. They were not yet ready to break the habit of making sure we were ready to host the people of God. People began to fill our new building with joyful music, waving palms, and celebratory spirits. In between worship experiences we held a brunch with those perfect little quiches you can stuff right into your mouth. The congregation was abuzz with excitement. It was a high time, a heyday of relief and joy.

Very few people knew that just a week earlier, we had walked into a flood in the sanctuary. One of the pipes under a sink in an area we hadn't remodeled had sprung a leak. It had filled our brand-new sanctuary's carpeting with water and damaged some of our sound equipment. It also filled our property team leaders with frustration and angst.

We had waited so long and journeyed so far. I am not someone who uses devil language on the regular but this time I did not resist. "Not today, Satan!" I proclaimed as we splashed through the building. It seems that resistance does come with doing God's will. Why else would the Apostle Paul have needed to remind the church in Romans 8 that neither powers nor principalities can separate us from the love of God in Christ Jesus? Pushback is part of the process of saying yes to God.

Yet somehow God even worked through that flood for our good. While the mega fans blew on our carpeting, the Holy Spirit blew on our hearts. Somebody said, "Well, the place needed to be baptized before we opened to the world." Perfectly put! Just like the synoptic gospels tell us that Jesus was baptized after his time in the wilderness, so we had been baptized after our time in the cafetorium. That flood became our sign that we were ready to open for divine business.

We put out a press release to invite media coverage for the big launch day. Sure enough, the local paper sent a photographer and one of our TV stations sent a reporter. When Jakob Brandenburg, the reporter, arrived, we tried to paint the whole picture for him about who we are, who we had been, and what we felt called to be about in our community. We even gave him a heaping plate of little quiches. But you never know how these news stories will turn out. Somehow, Jakob captured us perfectly. You can find the story on the Internet.[18] After the story aired, I thanked him for creating such a beautiful segment. He told me that he was glad our community had a church like ours.

Following our relocation and relaunch, our church became known anew as the church to call for community needs. I think that is because we don't just talk about helping the community, but we live it every single day. You may remember that when we were considering the purchase of the new building, we did a survey of area nonprofits to see if any needed better or more affordable space. We now host seven nonprofit organization partners operating out of our Connection Center, which is about 10,000 square feet of our building. Hosting means that they pay a below-market value to lease our office space. That includes utilities and even high-speed Internet if they need. Also, besides offices for each organization, our common areas are open to any of our partners by appointment. That means you are as likely to find a Big Brothers Big Sisters board meeting in our fellowship hall as you are a Bible study.

From counseling to mentoring for kids to support for cancer patients, a lot of community resources are housed on our campus. Our congregation's uber-involvement in the community, plus the fact of the Connection Center make us well known for serving our neighbors. Though we have much larger churches in our area, the city manager's office calls us when they need something. The school district calls us when they need help. The food bank calls us when they need support.

---

[18] https://www.cbs7.com/content/news/113-year-old-church-celebrates-Palm-Sunday-new-building-508573981.html

Recently, an attorney in town asked if we would host an adoption event for a dozen families. It's not that we're fancy, it's not that we're sleek, it's that we're ready and eager to host and serve, in any way possible.

Because of our congregation's innovation and God's faithfulness, when we opened in our new location, our church was postured to serve in ways exponential to our size. That's why when our city sustained the trauma of a mass shooting, our church helped to lead the way in recovery.

On a beautiful Labor Day weekend Saturday afternoon in 2019, a gunman ripped through our town, driving and shooting. He killed seven, wounded twenty-nine, and traumatized thousands. He was then killed by law enforcement. The gunman drove within a block of our church and within two blocks of our home.

That afternoon, Joe and I got the call to go to the hospital where we serve as volunteer chaplains. The hospital staff needed clergy to be with families waiting for word of their loved ones. We told our children not to go outside for any reason. Then we headed on our way, driving past blockades throughout the city that had been set during the search for the shooter.

We joined other pastors in doing our best to be a peaceful presence in the midst of the nightmare. We sat with people in deep shock. I used the best Spanish I could muster to pray with a stricken grandmother. Joe held a baby while his mother was in surgery. We walked people to the bathroom, staying with them so they would not feel alone. We watched surgeons hug police officers after working on one of their own. We heard devastating news being brought, over and over again.

Joe and I walked out of the emergency room hours later. A television news team was set up across the street and they captured us leaving. When some of our community leaders saw us on the news, they started texting us: *How can we help?* We told them we didn't know then, but we would soon. First, we needed to get ready for worship the next day. I scrapped my previous sermon and rebuilt it. I rested a bit and got up the next morning with a question on my mind: "How can the church bring Jesus' love to our community in this awful time?" I shared this question with the congregation, and prayerfully, we committed to be who God had called us to be.

Because our congregation had already said "yes" to God in less dramatic yet small, faithful ways in recent years, we were ready to serve. Joe and I led the planning of the community prayer vigil just a day after the shootings. We got back to all those people who had said they would help and put them to work. Relying on our partnerships with other churches and organizations, we called together pastors to pray, artists to offer poetry, music and dance, teachers to facilitate a chalk art mural, city leaders to speak, and most of all, the community to mourn. Thousands of people gathered on our university's campus to do just that.

The following day, our church's cooks got busy baking. We delivered hundreds of homemade cookies and cards to our hospitals, our post offices, our police and fire stations, and our wrecker services. We prayed with mail carriers and emergency room doctors. We brought cookies to all the businesses that were affected. We who were hit by a mobile murderer became a mobile movement of love.

A few months later, through the Department of Public Safety, our church sent cards to all of the victims and their families. We invited them to a dinner so they could meet one another. Working with sister churches through our ministerial alliance, we provided a meal of all the best church comfort food. We met at a community park's indoor pavilion, so that we were as accessible as possible, with no religious barriers. We promised no press, just love. I watched as people who had endured the unimaginable met others who understood completely for the first time. Healing was slowly and surely coming.

Just a week after the shootings, our city leaders began wrestling with what our community needed in order to heal. They started by holding meetings to coordinate resources for our community's recovery over the long haul. They were trying to figure out ways to respond for the healing of a traumatized town. But the meetings were held in a courtroom, which made a feeling of teamwork difficult. One of our church leaders was attending those meetings and she offered our church as a meeting place for the next time.

Of course! That's why we had converted the former dialysis lab into a fellowship hall and covered the large scale over with carpet. Not just so we could share a congregational meal every so often with our church, but so we could bless those outside our walls in need of blessing.

We didn't know it when we moved in five months previously, but we had repurposed ourselves and this building so we could host every conceivable public service organization in town over the next year. Leaders of those organizations included two pastors, members of law enforcement, and representatives of disaster relief and mental health. They met biweekly until the Family Resiliency Center was born. The FRC is a state-funded agency that offers free walk-in counseling and all kinds of support to anyone affected by the shootings. They especially provide incident debriefings and special mental health trainings for first responders and their families. Our community was able to birth the FRC because we were able to meet, and we were able to meet because our church had let God rebirth us just a few months before.

During the COVID-19 pandemic, our church hosted the community's one-year anniversary memorial as a drive-in service in our parking lot. Clergy from eight faith traditions were present to lead us. Fire trucks and police vehicles gathered in our lot. Staff from the Family Resiliency Center gave all first responders and families of victims a yellow flower. The music was from the Cassatt String Quartet, a New York-based group our church partners with when they are in town helping our school district. They offered their own arrangement of Amazing Grace just for this occasion. It was a moving service. But nothing could compare with the message God sent in the sky.

No rain was coming down as the sun began to set over our parking lot. Nevertheless, a rainbow appeared in the sky just above our building. We worship leaders couldn't see it as we faced away from the building and toward those gathered in the parking lot in their cars. But people began to text me. I could hear my phone buzzing but ignored it. I didn't want to be distracted from leading the service.

Then a stranger I didn't know got out of her car to come tell me: "Pastor, there's a rainbow over the building." Sure enough! When I turned around and looked up, there it was, a beautiful rainbow, seemingly out of nowhere. They could see it—those firefighters and police officers and the grieving families and caring neighbors. They knew that God was and is with us. What a gift to be a vessel for that kind of God!

The more integrated into the community our congregation becomes, the more our desire grows to be useful to our rainbow-giving God. Our exercises of compassion have developed a reflex in our leadership to perpetually ask our community, "Where does it hurt, and how can we help?"

In 2020 when thousands of unaccompanied migrant children came to our Mexican border, 1,200 of them were housed in an oil field camp just a fifteen-minute drive from our church. One of our congregation members was actively involved in an organization working to care for the kids. She asked if we could help. That was a yes!

Our church became a temporary warehouse for community members bringing craft and recreational supplies so these kids could have an uplifting way to spend their days of waiting. Pastor Joe went through the red-tape steps to be able to deliver those supplies personally to the children from our community and our congregation. That powerful experience made us hungry for more ways to help. We are now a winter shelter for the city, an occasional conference center for the school district, and a regular interfaith worship space for our domestic violence shelter. Who knows what's next? I think when most people ask for our help, they don't realize that we are not a great big church. We just smile because we know we serve a great big God!

In Their Words **by Tracy Austin**

I came to this church because of the Connection Center, the nonprofit organization wing of the church. I was leading a coalition in response to the mass shooting in our area. Pastor Dawn offered the community room (fellowship hall) for our meetings. It was comfortable, and not churchy. The Connection Center is what got me in the door to this church!

Just to be clear, I would not have stepped foot into the downtown church. Once I got in, I might have been successful, but I could not have gotten in the door. It was too traditional-looking and scary. My past history in the church, with the way people treated me because of the LGBTQ+ part of me—well, I just couldn't have done it.

I had a skewed perception of what Christians were. I would meet people serving in the community from Connection and I'd be thinking, "They're really kind; how can they be Christians?"

That's really how I felt. But after being in the building for those community meetings, and the ceiling didn't fall in, I decided to put my toe in the water. My husband and I argue about whose idea it was to come to worship at the church. Let's just say it was God's idea! I always think that's one good thing that came from the shootings. I found my church family.

When we started attending Connection, we found that what they were saying out in the community was actually true: you are accepted! Connection has given us the opportunity to belong. It's such a gift! It's changed my life in so many ways. I'm much less materialistic. I don't care if I'm driving a nice car; I want my money to go to the ministry here instead. I actually talk to God all the time now as a friend. And I tell people about this church. Because the love, the authentic love, I experience in this congregation is just amazing.

CHAPTER 12
Drive-In Church

We enjoyed our new-to-us building for nearly a year before the COVID-19 pandemic hit. Our last "normal" Sunday before the pandemic was March 15, 2020. Our attendance that day was way down as people were already concerned about the virus hitting our area. We put the full services up on Facebook live for the first time. At one point in the sermon, I made a point to look at every face there, to behold their presence, because I sensed we would not be back together for a long time, maybe ever, in the same way.

I told the congregation about my father who had polio as a six-year-old boy. One of his earliest memories is of the women of the church being gathered at the door outside his hospital room, praying for him. Joe and I challenged the church to be that kind of presence for others as COVID-19 unfolded among us. We determined together to be the church that stood beside others and prayed with them, giving our children memories of what faith looks like that would last a lifetime.

When school went online, the first thing our church did was open our parking lot to families who needed to use our excellent Wi-Fi. One day as I watched a family pull up in the lot to use it, it occurred to me that our parking lot might be able to be used for worship services. If we were offering it to the community, why not offer it to ourselves? When I got home that night, I discovered that Joe had the exact same thought. He remembered a Disciples of Christ church in Florida that was doing drive-in worship every Sunday of the year. We googled them and, sure enough! Still doing it. You do not ever have to go this stuff alone. Some church somewhere can help you out!

Joe is a quick study on all things techie, so he started researching. We called a mid-week Zoom church board meeting and laid out our seemingly crazy plan. Our board is used to wild adventures (see previous chapters), so they were up for it. What started as a stop-gap measure continued for fifty-nine Sundays. Drive-in worship shaped our ministry from that point on.

Drive-in worship meant people were more comfortable coming to worship. Folks who had mobility issues getting in and out of cars were grateful for the respite, as were their caregivers. It was easier in some ways to just drive in and have worship brought to them in their cars. Our LGBTQ+ community increased as people could check us out before they had to be so seen. And people whose own churches were not being very careful with health precautions came because they felt safe and had their concerns respected.

Many of our own congregation also loved coming to church casually. They brought their dogs like crazy. We even had a "Bring Your Dog Sunday" that was a hoot. Honking became the new "amen." People who were quarantining could still come to church, as long as they stayed in their cars and kept to themselves, and we could lay eyes on them and see they were alright. Folks could ask friends to meet them in the parking lot and introduce them to our church, as well as get to see their buddies, in a safe way.

We kept everything online but encouraged everyone in the congregation to at least try drive-in worship, because we knew it was changing our church in ways we would not be able to explain or replicate for those who missed out. Until you have seen people being baptized in a horse trough in your church's back parking lot, with people honking their hallelujahs, you just can't imagine what you're missing!

From Joe

"Change produces change." Coming out on the other side of our relocation, our congregation is more able in several ways. One gift we have acquired is adaptation.

We never skipped meeting in person when the pandemic hit. We had been in our building for a year and were ready to shut down like every responsible faith community the week we got the news. Then the idea hit us to leverage our space and move to drive-in worship in our parking lot. We decided it on Monday, and made it happen on Sunday. We had the right amount of parking space. We had mobile equipment. We had technological and A/V experience. We had the Spirit of trying new things.

We had prepared for relocation by planting seeds of change. We had worshiped in alternative locations for the years leading up to our move. And, during our transition, we had worshiped out of a trailer for 15 months, setting up mobile sacred space in a gymnasium. We all get used to things, and churches more so than most other entities, but our relocation process gave us an advantage when the pandemic hit. We were familiar with adapting to a changing environment. This has spilled over into many aspects of our ministry. The momentum behind "Let's try something new" has become greater than the force of "This is the way we've always done it." When that balance shifts, maybe it will be time to move again.

Drive-in worship made us the can-do church. We had a parking lot parade for our 2020 graduates after worship one day that brought out a media extravaganza. We hosted multiple community events from our parking lot like the United Way kick-off campaign. We held Christmas Eve services in the parking lot with a strolling string quartet and electric candles for "Silent Night." We even did a wedding! We've acted as consultant for small to huge churches trying to do similar things in their parking lots or even at drive-in movie theatres. I don't know if we would have had the imagination to conceive of doing worship in this unusual way if we had not already had so much practice thinking outside the box. I do know that made it a whole lot easier.

Easter Sunday 2020 came with fifty mile per hour winds. It was the most unusual and memorable Easter Sunday of my ministry so far. We greeted guests in the parking lot with a masked deacon giving each car a roll of wrapped toilet paper. On the TP was the message, "Hallelujah! The stone has been ROLLED away!" Toilet paper aisles were still empty in our grocery stores. But one of our church members owns a small office supply store and she was able to order some for us. People were chuckling all morning. It was my favorite Easter gift ever.

We borrowed the drum major stand from one of our local high schools for that literally High Holy Day. I was up to be the preacher. I climbed the ladder eight feet into the air and held on for dear life. The winds were howling! Would you believe I had worn heels that day? After one practice run up the ladder I ran home and grabbed some flats. I made it back with enough time to say a quick prayer and climb the ladder. While the wind pelted me, I held on to the railing and let the Spirit's own wind bring some good news. Having the gospel to share made far more lasting difference than anything else I could give the congregation, even more than a roll of toilet paper.

With drive-in worship came new ways of thinking about our outreach ministry. We began "Monday Meal Day" to provide meals to groups most affected by the pandemic. Meals went to our hospital staff working on the COVID floors several times, and also to our sheriff's office, our domestic violence shelter, the Boys and Girls Club staff, the juvenile detention center staff, and many more. We shifted our summer lunch feeding ministry from indoors where kids sat down with us to a delivery-on-the-porch style. We wrote hundreds of cards to leaders in our community feeling the burden of crisis and to teachers serving on the front lines. And we made masks—many, many masks—because our hospital staff and other front-line workers needed them before they were commercially available. We hosted four blood drives and three vaccination clinics, and became a COVID-19 testing site. We did even more outreach than normal, just all in a different way to be as safe as possible.

Every service we had was also online. But we decided that online was not our first priority; offering a safe, in-person experience was. Nonetheless, we gained new members of our church family who joined with us from afar. Folks from other cities and even other states sent in offerings of gratitude for the spiritual encouragement we provided.

We found that checking us out online was a comfortable way for many to test the waters first, before being vulnerable enough to come in the flesh. We added members who worshiped only online for a while, and then came to join us in person when they were ready. And still, we have folks who mostly worship online, but very much consider us their church. How people attend church is in flux during a time of technology explosion plus the pandemic's change of people's preferences. Our church's goal remains the same: "connecting you to Christ and community." In-person connection, following Jesus together, loving each other, and serving others in Jesus' name are the main things.

Though they didn't get COVID-19 at church, as best we can tell, many of our folks did get it. If we knew you had it, homemade meals were on your doorstep along with cleaning products, hand sanitizers, and tissues. Our elders regularly checked in with all of our active participants to see how folks were. We developed a way to check on our oldest members weekly instead of our previous monthly schedule. And the best thing we did was something we pastors didn't organize at all: the congregation instinctively took care of their pastors.

I developed some anxiety over leading the Lord's Prayer during this season. When you lead the Lord's Prayer and can hear voices saying it with you, it's comforting. If you stumble on a word somewhere, the congregation says it for you, and you just pick right back up. But saying the Lord's Prayer hearing only my own voice was daunting. It didn't sound right no matter how many times I did it. Do we say debts, trespasses, or sins? I knew it was debts and debtors, but without the congregation's voices, I hesitated.

Many times in Bible studies over the years, I have pointed out that the Lord's Prayer starts with "Our" Father, acknowledging that we do not pray it as individuals. Even if I am alone, when I say "Our" I know it's more than just me gathered to pray. Having to say the Lord's Prayer by myself became my symbol of all of the struggle of the pandemic. I could've been teased mercilessly for my fumbles on the prayer—"We've got a pastor who doesn't know the Lord's Prayer!"— but instead, the congregation was merciful and supportive, and took good care of their pastors every step of the way.

They honked with love and cheer at anything worth "amening" in our announcements, sermons, or music. We received regular notes of encouragement. People prayed for us. Our leaders urged us to take some vacation time and when we did, we discovered an envelope of "fun money" gift cards had been sent to us in the mail. When we ourselves contracted COVID, a hot meal was on our porch every evening. One of our dear elders filled in, memorizing the sermon I'd prepared and sharing it word for word with the congregation. The congregation didn't expect us to be superhuman and regularly asked how we were.

Because of pandemic travel restrictions, Joe and I missed our sabbatical, which should have been the summer of 2020. Sabbatical is a common practice among churches in our denomination. After every six years or so, clergy are given around three months to rest from any work related to the church. This helps keep ministers healthy, and churches too. Our leaders insisted that no matter what, Joe and I would take sabbatical in the summer of 2021. Sure enough, Joe and I each took three months off that summer, two months of which were together. We received not a single phone call from the church during that time. They managed beautifully. People still came to worship and stayed involved in outreach. New leaders emerged. Our pulpit was filled by capable preachers from throughout the Christian Church (Disciples of Christ). Not only did Joe and I receive needed rest and renewal, but the church received a powerful affirmation of their own strength and future.

Joe and I led a lot of changes during the nearly seven years before we took a sabbatical. Some might have wondered if the congregation was fully functional without our leading, or if they were truly dedicated to the path we had chosen together. The answer was a resounding "Yes." Yes, they took care of each other; yes, they kept making room for new people, and yes, they kept offering our resources in service to gospel work in our community. Connection Christian Church is who we are because of God's grace, not because of its clergy. Our sabbaticals proved that.

Joe and I feel spoiled to be pastors to this church. Many of our leaders commented that had we not moved before the pandemic, we likely would not have had the momentum left to survive it as a congregation. Their clear-eyed discipleship is a gift to their pastors. That included their common sense about the coronavirus. They have not been in denial about the seriousness of the pandemic. They have lamented changes we needed to make but did not resist them. We are Team Connection all the way. Being on the same page, not about everything, but about the main things, is a rarer feeling than you might think for a pastor-and-flock relationship. A pandemic fully brought that out, an unexpected miracle.

In Their Words **by Lezlie Veach**

I began this journey during the most difficult time of my life. I met Pastor Dawn shortly after my mom passed away. As we were getting to know each other, she checked in on me several times. Once, she shared an encouraging message about how to get through the holidays after the loss of a loved one. It was these simple connections that piqued my interest in Connection Christian Church. Then my sister had what was supposed to be a routine surgery, but this surgery resulted in a difficult three month stay in hospital and a devastating loss to our family. It was seven months and ten days after my mom died that I lost my only sibling—my dear sister.

The first time I attended a service at Connection Christian Church was my sister's memorial service. I was completely heartbroken and lost but I had been reaching out to God a lot during the previous two years. God was there for me and was calling me to open up to him. It was during my brokenness that I began to say yes to God. God was healing my heart and helping me make positive changes in myself so I could be there for my family.

At first, when I began to learn about all the things Connection is involved in, I felt very protective of "my" time. I think my perception was I didn't have the time or energy to give. After I joined Connection, the volunteer opportunities started coming. Then I found myself saying yes, especially during the COVID-19 pandemic: when there was a need for volunteers to work at the West Texas Food Bank, when there was a blood drive, when there was an opportunity to attend a fundraiser for Meals on Wheels, or when there were opportunities to participate in special events at the church. Suddenly, I was no longer worried about "my" time. Instead, I began to feel better and look for more ways to be of service to others.

These past years during the pandemic I have seen people in our congregation reach out in amazing ways. They have prepared and taught Sunday school and children's church, even online. They have sewn masks for medical staff, cooked meals for first responders, delivered lunches for the kids at La Promesa, and visited the Ector County Youth Center inmates to offer hope and love. The list of people saying yes, no matter their circumstances, goes on and on.

CHAPTER 13

Surprised to Thrive

Even though we relaunched as Connection Christian Church nearly three years ago, we are not back to business as usual. It would be easy to settle in and get comfortable after all of the change our church has navigated. But we did not take all these leaps of faith to get complacent now.

A church is a lot like a body of water. A river needs fresh water to come into it, and it needs to pour water out of itself in order to remain alive and thriving. "I came so that you may have life and have it to the fullest," Jesus says in the gospel of John.[19] That "you" in Jesus' words is a "y'all," which means something to us in West Texas. Abundant life is a community experience.

That's why together our church leadership is asking: *How will we grow, how will we love, how will we serve, how will we keep changing to follow Jesus more closely so the Holy Spirit can keep flowing through us?* As we prayerfully question, we are tending three tributaries to keep the river flowing: intentional discipling, widening our welcome, and deepening our community connections.

Growth in discipleship means intentionality. These days, being part of a church is no longer necessary to check off the "I'm a good person" box in our society. It's no longer a proven ingredient to network for your business or your reputation. I know many people who consider themselves Christians but don't have a particular church home. So do you. I know folks who are living their lives without any religious commitments, but occasionally dip into spiritual practices like yoga or nature walks for their soul's nurture. So do you. Scholars say the United States, Canada, and Europe are becoming "post-Christian"

---

[19] John 10:10.

societies. In other words, being a Christian is less and less a part of society. The rise of the "nones," those who claim no faith category, continues to be newsworthy. In 2019, those who claimed "none" as their religious preference became the second largest religious identity in the United States, surpassing Southern Baptists and only ceding to Roman Catholics.[20] We can no longer assume anyone has the basic foundation for a biblical or Christian faith. Nor can one hour a month, which now seems to be the average church attendance, possibly shape someone in following Jesus for a lifetime, much less for the first time.[21]

Enter intentional and winsome discipleship opportunities. For our church, this starts with an annual Bible reading plan, refreshed every year. Our expectation and invitation is that our congregation members are reading scripture every week, as well as working on memorizing a scripture verse. We've had a Year of the Bible as an introduction to the whole big thing. We've had a Year of the Gospel, where we dive deeply into the life of Jesus. We are currently enjoying A Fruitful Year, based on the fruits of the Spirit in Galatians. We have preaching series within these year-long reading plans, to give new folks a place to hop on. But always the intention is that our congregation is reading the scripture in manageable bites for a foundation in God's Word.

From there, we give every participant in our church a place of connection. We are not a church where it is easy to come and go. When you're here, we make a point to notice. Connection can be both voluntary and involuntary. How do you connect involuntarily? Through our shepherding groups, led by church elders. In the Christian Church (Disciples of Christ), elders serve alongside pastors as spiritual leaders for our church. Each elder is assigned about ten households to connect with each year. Phone calls, notes, texts, and in-person visits and events help keep the "sheep" connected to their "shepherd." When a powerful winter storm hit our state in 2021, the shepherds called their flocks. We knew quickly who needed help and offered it immediately. We hear pretty regularly that this care our church offers

[20] "In United States Decline of Christianity Continues at Rapid Pace," Pew Research Center, October 17, 2019, https://www.pewforum.org/2019/10/17/in-u-s-decline-of-christianity-continues-at-rapid-pace/

[21] "Religious Landscape Study," Pew Research Center, accessed March 11, 2022, https://www.pewforum.org/religious-landscape-study/attendance-at-religious-services/

is the first time someone has really felt like a part of a community. Receiving nurturing first, without taking initiative, is a step for most in our congregation toward choosing to be voluntarily connected to a place of growth and service.

We also have Jesus-focused small groups that people can choose to join. They meet as Bible studies, service teams, music groups, and age-related fellowship and support communities. Our goal is for 75% of our church to be plugged into one or more of these groups, and for the other 25% to be thinking about it. From these purposeful relationships comes the giving and taking of discipleship. You may know that the part of Texas where our congregation lives is as flat as it can be. And our trees are few and far between. We may be a three-hour drive from the Mexican border, but we like to say we can see it from here. In a similar way, we aren't yet like Jesus, but through our small group camaraderie and challenge, we can see Jesus from here. As one study group participant mentioned to her group recently, "Has your life changed since you've been going to this church? Mine sure has." To which another person replied, "Maybe I'm just getting older? But yeah. I feel it too."

For us, discipleship means both personal change in individual lives, and systemic, societal change. That includes raising up anti-racism advocates. George Floyd's murder was a tipping point for our country. It was for Odessa, Texas, too. Two marches were organized by community leaders and attended by hundreds of people, including many from our church and their pastors. Joe and I both preached about racial justice, not for the first time, mind you. Like many predominately Anglo congregations during the COVID-19 pandemic, we developed a study team that met via Zoom to study about being anti-racist. In one of our meetings, we invited the Rev. Gene Collins to speak. Rev. Collins is an African-American Church of Christ pastor and a beloved friend to our church. He grew up in Odessa on the "southside" before integration. In fact, he was the first baby of color born who was allowed to stay with his mother up on our county hospital's floors. Prior to that time, all patients of color were kept in the basement of the hospital, whether they were newborn babies and moms, or an elderly man with pneumonia. Rev. Collins spoke to us about the pride and the pain of being Black in our own community.

His testimony galvanized our group to do something to educate more of our community about the history of race in Odessa. We developed an "Anti-Racism Tour" for our city. We stopped at the public hospital, the courthouse, and the previously segregated former high school. But the jewel of the tour was "The Flats." Now only a basketball court with an unfinished, fading mural on an old mechanic shop as its background, you would miss The Flats if you were just driving by. But for decades, from the 1920s to the 1970s, this was the center of Black life in Odessa. Rev. Collins made it come to life, and you could almost see the hot dog stand, the street musicians, and the hotel where the Harlem Globetrotters had stayed because they weren't welcome on the white side of town.

Some of those attending the Anti-Racism Tour began to hatch the idea of further developing this area so its history could be known to new generations. Now, our small anti-racism group is involved with a much larger community task force. We are working with local Black leaders to lift up the historical significance of The Flats in new ways, including the creation of a public art mural. And the Anti-Racism Tour is becoming an annual event.

Not surprisingly, as God opens our eyes to the truths many have known for a lifetime, the ethnic diversity of those joining our congregation is growing. We are widening our welcome. I am awed by the trust people of color are placing in our predominantly white congregation. They see us intentionally engaging racism, not shying away from the costs of becoming anti-racist and taking action beyond just talking about it. For us, social justice is about true evangelism, taking the good news out into the world around us, as well as hearing it for ourselves. We still have untold work to do to become a congregation that more fully embraces all of our community. We aren't who we're going to be—but thank God we're not who we used to be!

Our community connections, both online and in person, continue to transform us too. Since the pandemic, our online presence and sense of community over the Internet has been changing the way we think about church. We pay attention to who is joining us, and we reach out and engage them as their church home. Our presence extends widely through the livestreamed worship and study events we share. Yet what remains most important to us is that it makes an impact on lives locally.

Hyper-local is the way we roll. We are learning more and more about how to share the gospel in meaningful ways with our neighbors. Our community's needs have only grown, as has our congregation's generosity. Our partnership with La Promesa now means year-round food distributions and care. We are working with our school district to provide wraparound support for our incarcerated youth in creative new ways. Our public hospital has grown to depend on us for coordinating the faith community to support their efforts, including hosting vaccine clinics and blood drives. We continue to nurture the nonprofit organizations and staff in our Connection Center and find new ways to be a blessing through their work. Our church is always discerning where we can invest significantly and consistently to change lives with God's love in Jesus Christ through the church.

This eye on our community connections keeps us morphing to become what Jesus needs us to be in our neighborhood. After all, as the Apostle Paul says, we are servants of Christ and stewards of God's mysteries.[22] The good news keeps jumping out of our hearts and into walking the walk about Jesus.

Last week, a new guest came to worship at our church. She had been watching our services online after seeing an article in the local paper about our ministry with incarcerated youth. She took courage and came in person that day. She was hesitant, though, about taking communion. She asked one of our greeters if our church allowed her to receive it. When he said yes, she replied, "But you don't know anything about me!"

And he answered, "God knows it all and loves you anyway. And the rest of us are not very easy to offend." When this story got back to me, I praised God. That's the church thriving!

Intentional discipling, a wider welcome, and deepening our community connections result in changing lives. At last, our church's future is no longer foreboding. Instead, it's an exciting adventure, trying to keep up with Jesus' leading in our lives. The water keeps coming in and pouring out. This creek is overflowing its banks, right here in the desert.

---

[22] 1 Corinthians 4:1

In Their Words **by Jeremiah Ologhobo**

I have always identified as a Christian and loved being in the presence of the Lord most especially on Sundays. And because of my knowledge of the verse of the scriptures that says "not abandoning our collective gatherings, as is the habit for some," I have always made it a point of duty to be at service somewhere every Sunday when I am not working.[23] One of those Sundays was in September of 2019. I was having some car troubles, and did not want to miss worship, so I decided to walk to the closest church in my neighborhood at that time.

My mum had attended services at Connection Christian Church in the past, and she spoke fondly of Pastor Dawn, and how she had a sister-in-law who was a missionary to Ogbomosho in Osun state, Nigeria, my country of origin. Being an introvert, my plan was to sneak in, keep to myself, enjoy the aura of being in God's presence, and leave without being discovered. But Pastor Dawn found me, welcomed me with open arms to the church, and even invited me along with the congregation to volunteer at the West Texas Food Bank and other community engagements after the service. Many others welcomed me enthusiastically as well.

The congregation's excitement about service to our community is contagious. Their care for the community is inclusive, for all people. Pastors Joe and Dawn's willingness to speak the truth about current events, especially racial and civil rights, caused me to respect them a great deal. As the congregation followed the highest standards in the midst of the COVID-19 pandemic, that moved my respect for this church to an even higher level.

I had always loved the idea of volunteering, but my work schedule prevented me. Also, I had never been around a Christian gathering that took so much pride in volunteering and community engagement, so I stayed. I joined the church in 2020 and have been blessed ever since.

---

[23] Hebrews 10:25

CHAPTER 14

After

When we made the decision in 2017 to relocate, the most frequent comment we heard from folks who didn't attend our church was, "But we'll miss the bells!" The bells that chimed throughout the day from the church's bell tower downtown were a beloved tradition for those working in the businesses around our neighborhood. There was no denying it; the bells would be silent once we moved.

This was an important reminder that although these folks didn't participate in our church, its presence was reassuring to them, and they were centered in God in some way by the sound of our bells. Whatever we did going forward needed to be not only a general presence, but a chiming of a call to engage, and in a way that asked for more than a momentary ear.

By God's merciful patience and energizing power, that call is pealing through Connection Christian Church now. And we are getting those physical bells ringing again. They will sound on the outside what we are on the inside. When we made the move, adventurous Pastor Joe got up in the bell tower and took down all of the equipment. It was stored in our new building for three years. Two heavy equipment companies that normally work in the oil field volunteered to remove the array. It was quite a sight to see. We had to get city permission to block the streets off as they worked.

A master welder in town is now recreating a tower, soldering the array to it. Soon the bells of our church will ring again, with renewed purpose, for a nearly entirely new congregation, in our new location.

Once more the good news is a-going out, the news that God does some of God's most beautiful work among the too old, too late, too desperate, and too dead. I've seen it. I can testify. And not just in my own congregation. Maybe the best blessing of our transition is to be able to offer hope and help to other congregations who are struggling. We are regularly blessed to be in conversations with sister churches who are looking at radical changes so that they too can embrace hopeful futures. So many churches are rattling around in buildings that are costing them more than just money. Not all need to move, but many need to repurpose their space, if not relocate. Our leadership loves visiting with other congregations as they make prayerful decisions about their futures.

First Christian Church in San Angelo, Texas, sent a delegation from their congregation to check us out as they considered a visioning plan with their new pastor. They toured our new facility and met with leaders of our church. We were part of their discernment that led them to decide to stay in their vibrant downtown area. They've done a beautiful remodel to make more connection with their community. They are also merging with another congregation in town. Check them out![24]

First Christian Church in Abilene, Texas, came to visit us as they were making decisions about whether or not to relocate. We showed their leaders around town, visited our old location, had a meal in our new fellowship hall, and even got them to spend a little elbow grease helping us add chairs into our new sanctuary. They completed their own relocation in 2020 and are once again a thriving witness to their community. Now they are experiencing new life in a right-sized building with a new pastor. You can learn more about them too![25]

Other churches we have had the joy of chatting with on their journeys have taken their own creative approaches to reinventing themselves with God's help. Some are merging with other congregations, others have relocated, and another has decided to redevelop their outreach ministry right where they are. Now that about 60% of faith communities in the United States have less than 100 people participating in their congregations, many churches are well past the time for making changes that will sustain their witness for the next generations.[26]

---

[24] For more information, please see https://fccsanangelo.org

[25] For more information, please see https://fccabilenetx.com

[26] "Fast Facts About American Religion," Hartford Institute for Religion Research, accessed March 11, 2022, http://hirr.hartsem.edu/research/fastfacts/fast_facts.html#sizecong

I know it's scary. But, here in our eighth year, I wouldn't take anything for our journey now. A new corner at the intersection of Inclusive and Purposeful holds our church building, which also includes offices for seven vital community nonprofits. An entirely new generation of churchgoers now fills up our part of the body of Christ. Our worship attendance has more than doubled from where we began eight years ago, even in the COVID-19 pandemic, and is still growing nearly every time we gather, with guests coming to check us out. Three years after moving in, 70% of our congregation never worshiped in our downtown location. In our old location, a fourth of our income to meet our expenses came from our endowment; now our giving more than sustains our ministry. And our community knows our 116-year-old church as one of the best servants in town. Our congregation, and its pastors, are gloriously alive and primed for a vibrant future. For as Jesus' mother told us, nothing God says is impossible.[27]

Are you praying to see God transform your congregation? God's plan is still to reach this broken, beautiful world through people who follow Jesus together. We are here to help each other thrive, not just barely survive. We are here to go on grand adventures in faith and see what the Holy Spirit will do. We are here to say "yes" to the Lord.

I wish I could take you outdoors to sit on a cold folding chair on a hot July night. There, we might sing some worship songs and enjoy the divine Presence. We might look up at the stars and let our eyes adjust until we can see more than we could at first. Then, quietly yet firmly, I might tell you that God's blessings must come not only *to* you but *through* you to truly be divine blessing. And then, you might feel the nudge of God's calling to you. If you do, I pray you have the courage to say yes, even though you don't know exactly what that calling will entail. And if you do say yes, I encourage you to write your "yes" down in your Bible and date it. Because the headwinds may be strong, but you will always know that God really called you. That's all you'll need.

---

[27] Luke 1:37

Small Group Discussion Guide

Chapter I

Reflect:
Read Luke 1:1-3.

Imagine the author of Luke's gospel working to put the story of Jesus together in such a way that others could hear it and feel like they are meeting Jesus in his book.

Review the story your church has to tell. What is your church's faith story? Your pastor's? Yours? Where do they connect? What are the holy connections that have brought you to this moment together? How are you telling the story?

Chapter 2

Reflect:
Read Luke 1:5-18.

Zechariah and Elizabeth assumed it was too late for them to parent a child. That train seemed to have left the station.

What assumptions are you currently making about your church? What is your current narrative, or the story you tell as you describe your congregation ("we're small," "we're friendly," "we're dying")? Do you think it is too late for your church to be what God wants it to be?

What do you guess the next 5 years will look like for your congregation? How comfortable are you with your assumptions?

When's the last time you personally took a leap of faith? When's the last time your church risked something big for God? How did it turn out?

Chapter 3

Reflect:
Read Luke 2:41-48.

Jesus' parents were searching desperately for him. They could not possibly journey on without him.

How are you seeking Jesus in your life? In your church's life together? Are you willing to pause until you've found his presence? Where are you looking? What new places have you checked recently, or could you check?

Chapter 4

Reflect:
Read Luke 4:1-13

Jesus faced the temptation to please Satan. Hopefully the constituents you are trying to please have nothing in common with the devil himself. Nonetheless, if they distract you from God's mission for you, they must be rebuffed.

Who are you trying to please in the decisions you are making as a congregation? Which voices and factions are vying for your attention? How are you getting out of touch with people pleasing, and in touch with Jesus-pleasing?

Chapter 5

Reflect:
Read Luke 7:11-17.

Sometimes the news is almost too good to be true. God can raise the dead!

What is dead or nearly dead in your life? When have you received an unexpected resurrection? Were you searching for it, or did it just come?

We considered it a miracle that we were able to vote on selling and buying—at nearly the same amount—on the same Eastertide Sunday. What miracles have you seen lately? Do you believe they are possible?

Chapter 6

Reflect:
Read Luke 9:28-37.

Jesus was changed before the disciples' eyes, and they saw his glory. Then immediately the disciples just wanted to stay in that spot.

How do you feel about change? Do you have change fatigue, or is your tiredness more from resisting change? Do you see Jesus' glory as coming from things staying the same, or from change occurring?

Chapter 7

Reflect:
Read Luke 9:57-62.

"I have decided to follow Jesus, no turning back," an old hymn goes. Sometimes it is hard to give up what we leave behind to follow Jesus.

What would a letting-go-of-keys ceremony look like for you personally, or for your congregation? What authority or responsibility are you carrying that is no longer necessary? How are you giving yourselves room to release what is now behind you?

Chapter 8

Reflect:
Read Luke 10:1-12.

When Jesus sent the disciples out on mission, he told them to travel lightly. They were amazed to see that God provided for their needs as they journeyed.

What in-between time are you in right now in your life, or in your congregation? What is it like to not exactly know what will happen next? Which Bible stories honor liminal time as a spiritually important season? How might God work if you allowed yourself time in the cocoon, or the wilderness?

Chapter 9

Reflect:
Read Luke 10:25-37.

Jesus teaches that loving God and loving others is what following him is all about. It seems so simple until we have to go way out of the way to actually love well; until our convenience and resources are on the line.

How specifically does your congregation love one another? How do you love people with whom you disagree? How does your love for each other show up in times of tension or conflict? How do you love people and God with your financial resources?

Chapter 10

Reflect:
Read Luke 14:7-24.

Jesus sets an unusual and rarely-followed standard for who we invite to our table. We are to go and get those who were not initially invited to the party. If every church in town goes for the young, heterosexual, professional couple with 2.5 children, no one reaches the rest of the people.

How clear is your church's welcome? What needs to be done to open the door more boldly to people who need the love of God in Jesus Christ?

Chapter 11

Reflect:
Read Luke 23:44-49.

When others saw Christ's suffering, they went away. But according to Luke, those who knew and loved Jesus stayed through it all.

Where are the places of lament in your neighborhood? How are you staying with those who suffer instead of going away? What small opportunities in God's will are you saying yes to now? How might those lead to bigger opportunities to be a witness to your community?

Chapter 12

Reflect:
Read Luke 24:1-9.

Jesus' resurrection completely interrupted what the women expected to find at the tomb. But they adjusted quickly!

What did the pandemic interrupt for you personally or for your church? What new life has come from it? Where is there still loss and death? How, and how well, have you adjusted? How are you caring for your pastor(s)?

Chapter 13

Reflect:
Read Luke 24:13-32

The disciples who encountered Jesus on the road to Emmaus thought they had experienced his presence. But they weren't sure. Finally, they got a big enough nudge that they changed their plans!

What's a nudge you may be experiencing from God in your life or in your church? What would following that nudge cost you? What would it cost you not to follow?

Chapter 14

Reflect:
Read Luke 24:36-43

When Jesus appeared to the disciples, they were startled and frightened. When we see what God wants us to see, it may make us uncomfortable. What have you seen in this time of study and prayerful thought? Does it make you uncomfortable, like the disciples?

The scripture says that our disbelief may even come from joy at what God could do that is beyond our imagining. Consider what God may do through you and your church.